This book is presented to

_____

CHRISTIAN ATHLETES *VS* THE WORLD

A Christian Athlete's Guide to Conquering Challenges Worldwide

Vol. 1

What to Know Before You Go
DRAKE REED

COPYRIGHT© 2024. DRAKE REED. CHRISTIAN ATHLETES VS THE WORLD, VOL. 1: A Christian Athlete's Guide to Conquering Challenges Worldwide
ISBN: 978-978-60126-7-4

Scripture quotations marked, unless otherwise indicated, are taken from the Holy Bible: KJV, ESV, NIV, NLT, MSG and TLB.

Drake Reed's book titles are available for bulk purchase for educational, ministerial, business, fundraising, or sales promotion purposes. For further details, kindly contact info@drakereed.com or visit www.drakereed.com and www.christianathletesworldwidealliance.com

Printed in the United States of America

Published by

YPN Publishing and Media, LLC
Leading International Publishing and Media Group
30 N Gould Street, Sheridan, WY 82801 USA
3A/2B Kano Crescent Agbara Estate, LA, NG

Mobile: +2348023768604
Email: admin@ypnpublishers-media.com
Web: www.ypnpublishers-media.com
 @ypnpublishers
 @ypnpublishers
 Ypnpublishingmedia

DEDICATION

This book is dedicated to God and all athletes worldwide.

Whether you're actively walking with Jesus, rediscovering your faith in Him, or seeking a relationship with the Lord and Savior named Jesus Christ of Nazareth, this book is dedicated to you in the name of Jesus.

ACKNOWLEDGEMENTS

I extend my deepest gratitude to the remarkable individuals whose unwavering support, guidance, and encouragement have been pivotal in bringing this project to fruition:

Bishop Lelton Davis, Bishop Calvin Lockett, and Bishop Calvin Scott: Your wisdom, counsel, and spiritual guidance have been invaluable throughout this journey.

Pastors Sean and Erica Moore, Pastors Joey and Judy Salinas, Pastor Juma Nashon, Pastor Christopher Deletsa, Pastor Charles Radford, Pastor Tim Ramsey, Pastor Shawn Scott, Pastor Paul Scott, Pastor Robert Harris, Pastor Jonel Marcelo, Pastor Nathan Freind, Pastor Franklin Centeno, Pastor Anthony Franklin, and Evangelist Katherine Lee: Your prayers, encouragement, and unwavering faith have sustained me through the challenges and triumphs of this endeavor.

My parents, Carl and Daphne Reed Sr., your unconditional love, unwavering support, and faith in me have been the foundations of my strength and resilience.

My brother, Carl Reed Jr. Your constant support, belief in my abilities, and shared journey have inspired and motivated me.

My advisor, Dr. Krystylle Richardson: Your guidance and expertise, both as a professional and a woman of God, made this project a reality.

All of my coaches, teammates, and fans worldwide: Your steadfast support, encouragement, and belief in my vision have fueled my determination and commitment to excellence.

To each of you, your contributions have left an indelible mark on this project and my life.

I am filled with profound appreciation and gratitude.

PREFACE

Welcome to *Christian Athletes vs. The World: A Christian Athlete's Guide to Conquering Challenges Worldwide.* As you hold this book in your hands, you are embarking on a transformative journey—one that transcends the boundaries of sport and spirituality and delves deep into the heart of what it means to be a Christian athlete in today's world.

In the pages that follow, you will encounter stories of triumph and perseverance, of struggle and redemption, woven together with timeless wisdom and practical guidance. But before we dive into the depths of these narratives, allow me to share with you the genesis of this endeavor.

For years, I have walked the paths of both athlete and Christian, navigating the highs and lows, the victories and defeats. Along this journey, I was met with tremendous temptation and resistance and lost my way, only to regain my relationship with God at the conclusion of my playing career. I have been blessed to deliver this book to edify Christian athletes and keep them on the straight and narrow path, which has inspired me to embark on this writing adventure.

Christian Athletes vs. The World is not merely a collection of anecdotes or a manual for athletic success. It is a testament to the power of faith, a rallying cry for those who refuse to compromise their beliefs in the face of adversity, and a roadmap for navigating the challenges that accompany the pursuit of excellence.

As you embark on this journey with me, I encourage you to approach these pages with an open heart and a hungry spirit. May the stories ignite a fire within you—a fire fueled by faith, perseverance, and an unwavering commitment to victory.

Together, let us rise above the fray, conquer our fears, and emerge as champions—both on the court and in the arena of life.

CONTENTS

INTRODUCTION

What does it mean to be a Christian athlete in a world where the playing field is not only physical but also spiritual? How do we navigate the turbulent waters of competition, pressure, and doubt while remaining steadfast in our faith?

After over a decade of playing basketball professionally overseas in six countries and traveling to over 20 nations, I returned home only to realize that all of the trials and tribulations the Lord brought me through were being catapulted on my people at home in America. I also realized that overseas many of my fellow athletes suffer from depression, stress, mental health challenges, and identity crises. I've been writing this book in many forms for many years. I stopped and started writing many times. I knew this book could not be finished until my professional sports career was completely over, but when my career came to an abrupt end during the COVID-19 pandemic, my life and all that I thought I knew came to an abrupt halt. It was the first time in my life that I was forced to be still and face all that I believed in and had been exposed to. I put this book down about six months ago because of an intense time in my life. A woman of God prophesied to me that I must write a book concerning my experiences overseas to help others. I attended a Christian conference March 24-26, 2023, as well as attended my normal church services and another leadership conference at my home church. Needless to say, my eyes were opened to writing this book until completion under the guidance of my Lord and Savior, Jesus Christ of Nazareth.

Welcome, fellow athletes, warriors of faith, and seekers of victory! In a world where challenges loom like giants on the battlefield and where doubts and pressures assail us like relentless opponents, we stand as Christian athletes, ready to conquer and triumph.

As a seasoned athlete and devoted follower of Christ, I've faced my share of adversaries both on the court and in the arena of life. But fear not, for I bring you not just a playbook for success, but a manifesto for dominance—a blueprint forged in the fires of competition and illuminated by the unwavering light of faith. In these pages, we will embark on a quest unlike any other. We will explore the trials and triumphs of Christian athletes who have boldly faced the challenges of a world that often seems at odds with our beliefs. From the roar of the crowd to the solitude of the locker room, from the thrill of victory to the agony of defeat, we will uncover the strategies, the wisdom, and the unwavering faith that empower us to rise above, excel, and conquer our struggles.

But make no mistake, dear reader, this is not just a guide for athletes—it is a call to arms for all who dare to stand firm in their faith, boldly proclaim their beliefs, and shine as beacons of hope in a world desperate for heroes. This book is to help Christian athletes and coaches worldwide who play and coach domestically and internationally, whether they're from the United States or another country.

Christian athletes and coaches who travel to play and live in different cities, states and countries during high school, college, and professional levels will greatly benefit from this book. It is also extremely helpful to Christians who travel for business and to those who travel in general. This book is a must for any teacher, administrator and/or school board member of any school or district that serves Jesus Christ. It is also a must for any parent of a Christian athlete. Everything from what needs to be done before an athlete leaves the country (or state) to what to do during their season, the off-season, and retirement is in your hands. It covers the nuts and bolts of how to deal with the enemy, the challenges of racism, prejudice, territories, spiritual attacks, and practical matters as well as gives readers the ability to overcome these challenges more easily with Christ. Although I'm African American and write from this perspective, this book is also very beneficial to anyone, regardless of their home country, nationality, origin, sex, or ethnicity, who decides to play their sport in another city, state, country or travel to another country or state to live in general.

I also have a second nationality as a citizen of Mali, which I earned through researching my heritage, so I understand much of the West African perspective along with being well-versed in European cultures having lived in Europe for roughly eight years. As we stand at the intersection of athleticism and spirituality, poised on the brink of greatness, one question reverberates through the depths of our souls: How do we rise above, not just as athletes, but as ambassadors of Christ in a world that often seems at odds with our convictions?

Join me as we delve into the heart of this question, drawing inspiration from the stories of Christian athletes who have dared to defy the odds, to defy the skeptics, and to defy the very forces that seek to dim the light of our faith. This is a book that guides believers in Jesus Christ of Nazareth as well as those who may not be currently practicing the faith. Whether you don't believe in Jesus, haven't been introduced to Jesus, or have lost your way, this book will help you, too. My prayer is that as you continue reading, you will not only be informed but transformed into understanding all of what God wants you to know about what to be prepared for and what to do in your time away from home. You will be taught so much about the world and how it works by traveling, meeting people, and being exposed to different situations and information that the average person will not know during their travels. During this time of molding, being a young, impressionable person with a lot of talent, the world will do its best to latch onto you for its gain. It is my desire, and I believe the Lord's desire, for you to read this book to help protect yourself against unwanted pitfalls, wavering from the Lord, loneliness, fear, worry, and a myriad of attacks from the enemy. The key of *Christian Athletes vs. The World* is to help Christians leave home a Christian and return home a Christian, in the name of Jesus. So, tighten your laces, steel your resolve, and prepare to join the ranks of Christian athletes as we embark on a journey to conquer challenges worldwide. The game is on, and the victory is ours to claim!

In the name of Jesus, I decree and declare your journey to be blessed and filled with powerful testimonies to edify and save the souls of men and women worldwide. To God be the glory. Amen

If you're ready to win, turn the page.

Bible Translations Utilized

Keep these scriptures in mind during your entire experience:

Matthew 10:16-22

The Message (MSG)

"'Stay alert. This hazardous work I'm assigning you. You're going to be like sheep running through a wolf pack, so don't call attention to yourselves. Be as shrewd as a snake and as inoffensive as a dove. Don't be naive. Some people will question your motives; others will smear your reputation just because you believe in me. Don't be upset when they haul you before civil authorities. Without knowing it, they've done you and me a favor by giving you a platform for preaching the kingdom news! And don't worry about what you'll say or how you'll say it. The right words will be there; the Spirit of your Father will supply the words. When people realize it is the living God you are presenting and not some idol that makes them feel good, they are going to turn on you, even people in your own family. There is great irony here: proclaiming so much love, experiencing so much hate! But don't quit. Don't cave in. It is all well worth it in the end.'"

Jesus is letting His disciples know they will face persecution on their missionary trips. As a Christian athlete who travels to different places, you will be confronted with all sorts of challenges that the average person will experience, but they will be multiplied by visibility, pressure, financial gain or loss, mental or emotional strain, and spiritual confrontations.

John 15:18-21 MSG

"'If you find the godless world hating you, remember it got its start hating me. If you lived on the world's terms, the world would love you as one of its own. But since I picked you to live on God's terms and no longer on the world's terms, the world is going to hate you. When that happens, remember

this: Servants don't get better treatment than their masters. If they beat on me, they will certainly beat on you. If they did what I told them, they would do what you told them. They are going to do all these things to you because of the way they treated me because they don't know the One who sent me."'

Jesus explains this much to His disciples. As a follower of Christ, you will face hatred. And as an athlete, that hatred will be multiplied by the better player you are. Your light is already shining because of Jesus, and there will be times people will try to put your light out because they do not know God, so they will have little to no relent at times. Jesus will keep you safe, no matter the attack(s). Just understand that the attacks, no matter the kind, are the price of admission to being a Christian and an athlete.

1 John 2:15-17 MSG

"Don't love the world's ways. Don't love the world's goods. The love of the world squeezes out love for the father. Practically, everything that goes on in the world—wanting your way, wanting everything for yourself, wanting to appear important—has nothing to do with the Father. It just isolates you from Him. The world and all its wanting, wanting, wanting is on the way out, but whoever does what God wants is set for eternity."

To my fellow Christian athletes, does this passage not hold to our experience? When we get caught up in winning awards, money, fame, and so on, this can give us a high that replaces our desire for God to be present in our lives. It is good to have recognition, big money, and nice material things. However, be sure not to go overboard with pride and ego, but stay on track with your assignment from God. Within the following pages, we shall embark on an extraordinary expedition—a quest to conquer obstacles that span the globe, armed with the unwavering strength of our Christian convictions.

As we find ourselves at the crossroads of athleticism and spirituality, teetering on the precipice of greatness, one resounding question echoes within the depths of our souls: How do we transcend beyond mere athletes and become beacons of Christ's love in a world that often contradicts our beliefs?

Join me as we delve into the heart of this inquiry, drawing inspiration from the tales of Christian athletes who have dared to defy the odds, skeptics, and even the very forces that strive to extinguish the radiance of our faith.

Therefore, my fellow champions, as we embark on this collective journey, let us answer the call to greatness, embracing the forthcoming challenges and emerging triumphant—not only as victorious athletes but also as ambassadors of Christ. Together, let us illuminate the path for others to follow, exemplifying true strength in both body and spirit.

First Quarter

What you need to know before you leave the city, state or country.

1

Knowing Who You Are in Christ

"

The Lord is about keeping His Word.

– Drake Reed

"

"Lord, thank you for giving us all a concrete understanding of our identity in you. In the name of Jesus. Amen"

In my 20s, I found out how I was born; and in my 30s, I found out why I was born. When I began my sports career playing overseas at age 22, I thought I was a kid from St. Louis, Missouri, with a chip on his shoulder, ready to show the world who I was. I was a Christian at the time, but a baby Christian who knew little about the Word and even less about the world.

Like most great athletes, I had a chip on my shoulder, talked about all kinds of trash, and brought a level of intensity most people could not match. I was relentless on the court (known as a warrior to most) and played every possession like it was my last. As time went on from country to country, I learned more about history, cultures, religion, myself, and people from all walks of life taught me about life. I was put in situations that thwarted my belief in God, His Word, and His plans for me, and I could never put my finger on why Jesus was so important until the world hit me in the face. I went overseas to do big things on the court, see a bit of the world, and return home for a career in the National Basketball Association. I had it all planned out—how it would happen, why it would happen—only to experience roadblocks year after year. This is surely the plan for many American basketball players who travel to play in other countries, but the main thing we all find out is that we have to live in these countries with built-in barriers working against us.

There is very little that can mentally prepare you for the devastation you may witness in certain places outside of your home state or country. I've seen war, famine, depression, the dark arts, extreme racism, extreme pollution, and extreme poverty up close. I've also seen beautiful world wonders, met incredible people, enjoyed great foods and events, and enjoyed some of the greatest moments a person could ever dream of. Many international players struggle with loneliness, depression, and homesickness and are taken advantage of in a variety of ways due to being ignorant of how things work in other countries. Through it all, knowing who you are in Jesus Christ is fundamental to your walk overseas. If you know your relationship with Christ, His promises, and your role in the five-fold ministry, then your direction will be enhanced and challenges will be more understandable.

Once you've been baptized, you are filled with the Holy Spirit, and your relationship with Jesus Christ of Nazareth is fully established as He (the Holy Spirit) is residing inside of you. This is not some spooky thing that some may make it out to be; just know that you are now able to wield the authority that Jesus has given you through His Father, God Almighty, who resides in the 3rd heaven. For a young Christian who is between 14 and 25 years old, your understanding of this will probably be limited; this could be because of insufficient experience in putting God's Word to use. However, do not fear because, in due time, you will learn that God is who He says He is. Many Scriptures explain your relationship with Christ. Do not be fooled into believing that you need someone other than yourself to pray to God. You can exercise your authority in Jesus' name and call on Him.

> *Jesus considers us as a family (Matthew 12:46-50 MSG). In verse 50, Jesus states: "...The person who obeys my heavenly Father's will is my brother, sister, and mother."*

As Christians, we are all considered kin to our Lord and Savior, Jesus Christ. Yes, Jesus is all-powerful and mighty and has all of the positive attributes we've heard of for years. He still is humble enough to consider us family. No matter what situation you may be in, always know you can come to Jesus as a sister or brother. Speak respectfully to Him, but know that the love is sincere.

> *In John 15:15 New International Version (NIV), Jesus tells His disciples, "I no longer call you servants because a servant does not know his master's business. Instead, I have called you friends, for everything that I learned from my Father I have made known to you."*

Although we consider ourselves servants to the Lord, Jesus Himself lets us know He considers us friends; once again showing His humility.

> *Jesus says, "As the Father has loved me, so have I loved you. Now, remain in my love. If you keep my commands, you will remain in my love, just as I have kept my Father's commands and remain in His love" (John 15:9-10 NIV).*

> *"My command is this: Love each other as I have loved you" (John 15:12 NIV).*

All through the New Testament, Jesus spoke many powerful words that will give you a deeper understanding of what your relationship with Him is going to be like. His commands are based on love and behaving in ways in which someone who genuinely loves you will behave. Understanding your relationship with God will require you to read His word routinely, and like tying your shoelaces, the repetitiveness will eventually make it second nature. Secondly, knowing and understanding God's promises is very important. God has numerous promises that He continues to keep. Throughout the Bible, you will find several of these promises that will be of great benefit as you know and apply them to whatever situation may arise. For example, God promised that He would give Abraham's descendants the country called Israel; it was God's promise to Abraham. As time went on, there were all sorts of challenges, but God kept his word to Abraham, and generations later, Moses (a descendant of Abraham) led God's people to the promised land. Even when God's people turned away from God, didn't keep His commandments, and complained, God still pulled them through because of His promise to Abraham. One of the keys to any Christian's success is knowing how God's promises pertain to them. God promises His goodness, His protection, His provision, eternal life, and many more.

Think of any situation an athlete could be confronted with in their career. Let's say the community in which you're performing has turned against you; you're receiving all sorts of hateful social media messages; people are insulting you while you're out; and so forth. Well, this is a perfect time to call God on His promises, one of which is that He will keep His word. The prophet Jeremiah had an experience with the Lord which he shared in Jeremiah 1:5.

Here, God tells Jeremiah:

> "Before I shaped you in the womb, I knew all about you. Before you saw the light of day, I had holy plans for you: A prophet to the nations-that's what I had in mind for you" (Jeremiah 1:5 MSG).

So, here, God made it known to Jeremiah that He already has a complete understanding of him and his plight. Jeremiah had doubts about his ability to speak but God further informs Jeremiah:

> "God told me, 'Don't say, 'I'm only a boy.' I'll tell you where to go and you'll go there. I'll tell you what to say and you'll say it. Don't be afraid of a soul. I'll be right there, looking after you...'" (Jeremiah 1:7-8 MSG).

The Lord reassures Jeremiah, urging him not to doubt himself or fear his opposition because God is with him and will rescue him. God is clarifying Jeremiah's assignment. Later, in verse 12 of the NIV Bible, it states:

> *"The Lord said to me, 'You have seen correctly for I am watching to see my word is fulfilled.'"*
> *(Jeremiah 1:12 NIV).*

The Lord is about keeping His word. If you're having difficulty in your career or life, call the Lord on His word, because God says Himself that He is watching to see that it is fulfilled. Find the scripture that deals with the issues you're dealing with and just like when you do what your parents tell you to do and nothing happens, you can go back to them and say, "I did what you told me." God will see it through because He keeps His word. Do not be treacherous and try to use God's word to do your will, especially when you know your intentions are impure. God is not to be toyed with. Humble yourself, ask for forgiveness of your sins, do your best to repent, and remind God of His promises to you.

Moving on, the five-fold ministry consists of the Apostles, Prophets, Pastors, Teachers, and Evangelists. Each ministry is an integral part of the body of Christ, which is the church. Think of the body of Christ as different positions that make up a team. We were all born with certain gifts and assignments, which can be anything from the gifts of healing, prophecy, intercession, pastoring, and so on. This evidence of gifts will be as basic as being a good captain of a team, being a person who always tells your friends that something will happen and then it usually happens, or being extremely sensitive. These are basic signs of spiritual gifts that fit into different ministries. Knowing which ministry you belong to will typically be identified by elders in the church who have experience with these ministries and have a better connection with the Holy Spirit than a younger, inexperienced Christian may have. Knowing which ministry or group you belong to can also come about by asking the Holy Spirit through prayer and fasting. Either way, it is very important to know which group of the five-fold ministry you're operating in. So when the enemy comes against you, you will know what your gifts are and be better equipped to utilize them properly to do God's will in a given situation. This is no different than knowing your position as an athlete; different positions have different roles on the team. Within those positions, there are basic traits that players in that position have, whether it be a certain size, speed, mentality, etc.

This is much like the five-fold ministry: Apostles have gifts from each of the five positions. Prophets can prophesy, heal, and claim spiritual territories. Pastors lead the flock (like a coach leads a team). Teachers specialize in educating people about the Word. Evangelists are gifted in prayer as they intercede for others through prayer. Each person in a position has their gifts for a particular ministry, but people can also have a special anointing that goes beyond the usual limits of their position. An anointing is given to someone by God to supply a demand. For example, a pastor may be gifted in pastoring but be in an area that needs deliverance (exorcism), so the Lord may bless this pastor with an anointing to deliver the people of that area. Some pastors excel as great pastors overall while being anointed in their area of expertise. Does this sound familiar? Think of the shooting guard position in basketball where most shooting guards can shoot a high percentage from three-point range. However, there are those rare "shooting guards" who not only excel at shooting, but also possess the skills to handle the ball and play point guard when needed. Similarly, imagine a person gifted with a particular ministry who demonstrates abilities beyond their typical role.

Knowing your position in the five-fold ministry will prepare you for dealing with challenges that arise. This is life and you will be confronted with many challenges. Being on your own, away from loved ones, is a challenge in and of itself. Family and friends at home may know God, but time with them will be limited due to distance and different time zones. Knowing your gifts and how to use them will prepare you to defeat the devil. For example, if an evangelist is gifted in prayer, he or she wields more power in this area. Prayer breaks up hindrances and thwarts enemy plans. There could be dissension in your team or the organization could be coming against the players, but your actions and abilities of praying for hours at a time along with worshiping in gospel music can remove snares (tricks/schemes) from your teammates. This is no different from playing an opponent who specializes in fast break offense and your team struggles to play fast, but the coach makes a decision to play his faster players for this particular series and your team has more success. This is using your gifts properly.

If you're a prophet, then you may be extremely sensitive to unseen emotions from your coaching staff, teammates, or fans, so there will be times when you feel pressured or intense, depending on what's going on around you. Knowing you're a prophet/prophetess, you can be sure to have your prayer team shield you from other people's spiritual baggage. Not knowing your gifts or not utilizing them will allow your enemies to exploit your ignorance, as they'll do their best to keep you ignorant because they know if you use your gifts they are finished. This is how the enemy works both in the physical realm and the spiritual realm, as the enemy exists in both. Find your ministry and learn your gifts as soon as possible to stand strong against opposition.

Do not become arrogant about your gifts, because the reality is that your assignment for those gifts is hefty and the penalties for not using them properly are costly. Most experienced Christians will not boast about their gifts because they know the battles they've endured because of these gifts. Understand, also, that things come in God's timing. So, if you pray about identifying your ministry and nothing comes for a while, don't be dismayed, as it may not be the best time for you to know. God knows when to reveal life-changing information and He will reveal it when the time is right. You're an athlete, and for some athletes it may not be best to know if your gift is that of an apostle or pastor during your playing days as it could change what God wants you to experience during those days. Also, knowing this may open you up to more attacks during that time. Only God, or possibly a prophet or prophetess who is informed to do so by the Holy Spirit, knows the timing. Do not worry about not knowing your ministry gifts if they don't all come at once, as many realizations may come at set times in a person's life.

In the physical, many churches have developed spiritual gift assessments that help to identify a person's spiritual gifts and ministries.

The Pastors' Take on Knowing Who You Are in Christ

Bishop Lelton Davis
Mesa, Arizona, USA

Question

What is the importance of a person knowing who they are in Christ?

Bishop Davis' response

If you don't have your identity in Christ, you'll be lost in the world; you won't know your purpose. It's very important to understand your purpose. It's like getting in a car and driving but not really having a destination, after a while you're going to want to get out, like what's the point of doing all of this driving and we're just going in a circle and there's no purpose.

That's what I was like before I knew my calling and my identity in Christ. I was never really happy, I had money, drinking, and sometimes I chased women but wasn't satisfied with a lot of things. But there still was a hole in my heart that only God could fill. When a person does not have identity in Christ, he has no purpose in why he was born. Solomon, in his older years, realized that life is vanity without God. Once you know your identity in Christ, you realize what it is that God wants you to do or how you can allow Christ to work through you. Because greater is He (Holy Spirit/Jesus) that is in me than he (devil) that is in the world. Once I've (you've) realized who I (you) am called to be, I (you) won't let the world identify me because I know God has already qualified me and I'll just have to work to see what it is that God wants me to do here on earth.

Question

As athletes leave their families younger than most people, what is a way that an athlete can learn their identity in Christ sooner?

Bishop Davis' response

It's supposed to start in the home. That's why the Bible instructs us to train a child in the way they should go and as they get older they will not depart. Once you leave your parent's care or whoever raised you, that's when the world and the enemy will try to lure you and snatch you away.

> *"Train up a child in the way he should go, And when he is old, he will not depart from it" (Proverbs 22:6 New King James Version NKJV).*

Bishop Davis Continued

When I grew up, I identified as a basketball player. I had no backup plan. That was all I wanted, to be in the NBA or the NFL. I traveled the world and I did all these other things but if your foundation is not in God, you're not going to be protected when you're out there on the road.

You're not going to know who you are so you can easily get swept away with the temptations of life, the lust of the eyes that are never satisfied, the lust of the flesh does what feels good right now. You might get fame because of your gift and abilities on the basketball or football field, then you won't be prepared to understand how the enemy will use sexual temptation and sexual desires to lure you away from your purpose. If you're led by the flesh and not the spirit (especially if you're an athlete), you'll end up ruining everything that God put in you and everything that you built, because you won't know how to protect yourself with prayer and fasting. So, it starts with being trained in Christ. Having spiritual parents and having people who are praying for you is very helpful. This help arises when the enemy tries to lure you away from the very things that are protecting you.

Pastor Tim Ramsey
Luton, England, United Kingdom

Question

What is the importance of a person knowing who they are in Christ?

Pastor Tim's Response

I think identity is everything. When we come to Christ in 2 Corinthians 5:17, we're told that we become a new creation that has never existed before. You're almost like a new species; it's a new life, it's a new way, it's a new behavior, it's a new language. You have to learn it, you have to develop in it, you have to grow in it. What's transferred to us from the Lord himself is His nature, His identity. We take on His righteousness, we take on His peace, we take on His blood. Now the Father views us through the light and life of Christ.

> *"Therefore, if anyone is in Christ, the new creation has come: The old has gone, the new is here!" (2 Corinthians 5:17 NIV).*

Pastor Tim Continues

It's all about learning His way from His words, and when you do that it's almost like a journey of rediscovery. You're not so much finding yourself; you're finding yourself in Christ. It's a whole new identity, you're a new person, you're a new creature and you need to renew your mind in that regard. As you grow and develop, you discover and understand, as one of my favorite teachers used to call it, 'in Christ realities.' Who you are in Him, who you are in Christ, who you are in the body (church), and who you are in the plan and purpose of God. When you discover your identity, it assures you. It puts perseverance in you because things will come to challenge that identity. Things will come to take you back to your old way of doing things, your old way of thinking. When you're firm in your identity, part of a physical church family, your foundation is secured and you will not be swayed or moved by the challenges that life brings.

Question

How can a young person who is traveling to live in different cities, states, and countries keep from losing their identity in Christ?

Pastor Tim's Response

You have to believe and understand the reality of the fact that the Holy Spirit dwells on the inside of you. When you come into Christ, you become part of the body of Christ at large; however, you are a personal temple of the Holy Ghost. Christ dwells in you through His spirit, which is important because there may be times of isolation when you don't have your usual networks or comfort zones, your family, whether that's your blood family or whether that's your Christian family. So, when you're in these times of isolation, that's when you have to dig deep and in the fact that I'm (you're) alone because I'm (you're) not with my (your) family. However, Christ is with me (you). He said He'll never leave me nor forsake me. I have His spirit, therefore I have this 24/7 access to the Father, to the throne, to the kingdom, and to the things of God. It's easier said than done of course, but you've got to encourage yourself in these realities.

If I'm in a season where for six months I might not be able to go to a church and become part of a physical church family, it's difficult because I believe in the value of the church. I believe in the value of fellowship, but if there are seasons where those things are not at hand, God's still with you. Jesus is still with you and your private devotion will matter more in that season than it matters in another season.

Question

What happens to a person when they lose their identity in Christ?

Pastor Tim's Response

What happens generally is a thing the Scripture calls a backslide; you begin to transgress from the path that the Lord has assigned to you. That can start when your prayer life begins to ebb (fade) away, or you're not in your word (Bible) as much as you used to be. You can't carve out the time to get into the Word, so your private devotion begins to diminish. When you lose your identity, you start doing things that you know you shouldn't be doing. It's like the internal battle that the Apostle Paul said he had, "The things I know I should do, I don't do, and the things I want to do, I'm not doing." When you begin to lose your identity, you start to lose the battle more and more. There are times when people have spoken to me and said, "I don't even know who I am anymore, because I'm doing what I know I shouldn't be doing." Losing your identity can cost you your faith.

> *"What I don't understand about myself is that I decide one way, but then act another, doing things I absolutely despise. So if I can't be trusted to figure out what is best for myself and then do it, it becomes obvious that God's command is necessary. But I need something more! For if I know the law but still can't keep it, and if the power of sin within me keeps sabotaging my best intentions, I obviously need help!" (Romans 7:15-17 MSG).*

Pastor Juma Nashon
Nairobi, Kenya

Question

What's the importance of a person knowing who they are in Christ?

Pastor Juma's Response

It is critical that you know exactly what you've subscribed to and what kind of benefits are included in your subscription. It's important to know where you're coming from and where you're going. Your identity in Christ is very important because it is what transcends you from what the scripture says, "You have been translated from the kingdom of darkness into the kingdom of light." From where there are curses to where there are blessings, from where there is death to where there is life. So, your identity in Christ gives you that very child of God's identity. All of us are creatures of God, all of us are created by God, but it takes a deliberate, intentional decision for you to be a child of God for the scripture says, "Those who believed, who received and believed, He gave them the power to be children of God."

> *"For he has rescued us from the kingdom of darkness and transferred us into the Kingdom of his dear Son" (Colossians 1:13 New Living Translation NLT).*

> *"Yet to all who did receive him, to those who believed in his name, he gave the right to become children of God" (John 1:12 NIV).*

Pastor Juma Continues:

So, it's a choice, and therefore you gain the identity of being in Christ, a child of God and all the redemptive benefits can now be your portion. You have to understand when you are in a relationship with God, this is with Christ Jesus. There are no two ways. The Scripture says, "I am the way and the truth, and the life."

> *"Jesus answered, 'I am the way and the truth and the life. No one comes to Father except through me'" (John 14:6 NIV).*

Pastor Juma Continues:

You will get philosophies and persuasion but if anybody encounters you and is talking about anything, you have to be somebody that can relate to the scriptures. You are supposed to have the Word of God as the compass of everything as far as your encounters in a new place are concerned. Before you take any position, what is the Word of God? Yes, you may not have studied all of it, but at least you can refer to the Word of God. If you don't know the place (scriptures), you can at least reach a mature Christian. Simply ask, "This is what I am encountering, how should I go about it?" You need to get a mentor who can help you grow, and that mentor will always be your reference point in case you encounter something strange.

Pastor Christopher Deletsa
Lille, France

Question

What is your take on the importance of knowing who you are in Christ?

Pastor Christopher's Response

A lot of Christians don't know themselves; they don't know who they are. They are doing what they have been told to do, without knowing themselves. It is difficult to have intimacy with God without knowing yourself. There might be doctrines and principles that deal with individuals differently. That comes with knowing who you are, and it helps you to know how God talks to you, how to hear God's voice, how to interpret your dreams, and how to relate with people. Knowing who you are means that you know your weaknesses and you know your strengths. If you don't know your strengths and weaknesses, it pushes you back or takes you away from God, and you don't know how to ask God for help. Knowing yourself is very fundamental in God because you will now know this is how much God loves you and God is still using you. People believe Christianity is culture. It's not culture, it is not what we're brought in by our culture or our locations in our countries. It is the life of someone (Jesus) we are living, following after His examples.

Pastor Nathan Freind
Geelong, Australia

Question

What is the importance of knowing who you are in Christ?

Pastor Nathan's response

Identity in our Christian faith is crucial. You can't always rely on your home base to get you through your journey. There's got to be some self-awareness and some personal responsibility in taking on your faith and your faith journey to where you need to be able to take responsibility for it. Knowing your strengths and your weaknesses and your understanding of your Christian faith is crucial to your everyday walk. When I was playing basketball, I very easily could have been swayed into what the world offers because that's just what you do as an athlete. You finish playing a game and you go to the nightclub and party. If I didn't have my identity in Christ cemented like it was, who knows how easily I could've been swayed? You can't just rely on your local pastor from home to keep you grounded. You have to have your responsibilities in place, especially when you're traveling.

Question

With less time to attend Bible study, church events, and so on, how can a Christian athlete stay connected in their walk with God?

Pastor Nathan's response

What we have these days is the luxury of technology. You have to have this individual responsibility of what you do. Things that I always have near me are quick devotionals. They take five minutes, and it's a quick prayer and a quick thought. It's a quick meditation moment to spend with you and God. It's having those daily reminders to make sure that prayer is included, spending time in the Word. You can't take all your Christian mates (friends) and your church with you, but you can take your Bible with you anywhere you go, it's on your phone. As an athlete one thing that we have when we make it to a high level is that our discipline is through the roof; we know how to be disciplined. But all of a sudden, we don't apply the same thing to our Christian walk. When the two marry up nicely, that's when incredible things can happen and that's when God can use us in the greatest of ways. It's challenging, but it all comes down to whether we are willing to do the hard work ourselves.

Pastor Jonel Marcelo
Malay, Aklan, Philippines

Question

What is the importance of knowing who you are in Christ for someone who is constantly traveling to new places?

Pastor Jonel's response

If I talk about my personal life, my life was so devastated. My father was killed by my uncle, and my mother had mental issues. The importance of knowing Christ is very vital because when I experienced it (trauma) without Christ, I thought about killing myself and committing suicide, and then there you go, God found me. It is important because God is doing something that you don't know. Even if you are ordinary, you can be used by God and that's what happened to me.

For me, God gives us challenges to bestow Him. We must know God because He is the only answer.

Question

How can athletes stay connected to God with less time to be in church activities?

Pastor Jonel's response

One to five minutes of Bible reading, pray, and then read the Bible again. Don't forget that you can do all things through Christ who strengthens you. Philippians Chapter 4 verse 13. Remember who gives you strength. If you want to be a successful player, have time for God.

> *"I can do all this through him who gives me strength"*
> *(Philippians 4:13 NIV).*

Pastors Joey & Judy Salinas
Phoenix, Arizona, USA

Question

What is the importance of knowing who you are in Christ?

Pastor Joey's Response

Athlete or non-athlete, when you know who you truly are, you'll find that you fall less for the counterfeits in life. You think about all the times the devil tried to tempt Jesus at His weakest point, it was to try to take Him out of His identity, to get Jesus to strive for some kind of deity that was outside of Himself. The more you know yourself, the more you can own the characteristics that God says you can own, and the more you can embrace the skill sets, talents, and abilities you carry. The more you know you're loved, the more you know whom you're loved by. I feel you solidify your identity in those two things.

Pastor Judy's Response:

Reading scripture: the things that God says that we are a royal priesthood, that we are chosen, that we are loved, that we are conquerors, that we have the victory because He already won. The more we understand those things, the easier it is to recognize when something is not of God. When something is trying to tell us in our mind bad thoughts like, "You're not good enough, you're not going to make it, where is your God, where is your faith?" We can go back to what we have read in the Word, what we have gone through with God, building a history with God. He (God) gives us an inheritance as His children. What are those things? We get the fruits of the spirit, the gifts of the spirit. Those are all things that we get easy access to just to know our identity in Him.

> "But the fruit of the Spirit is love, joy, peace, longsuffering, gentleness, goodness, faith, meekness, temperance: against such there is no law" (Galatians 5:22-23 KJV).

> "A spiritual gift is given to each of us so we can help each other. To one person the Spirit gives the ability to give wise advice; to another, the same Spirit gives a message of special knowledge. The same Spirit gives great faith to another, and to someone else the one Spirit gives the gift of healing. He gives one person the power to perform miracles, and another the ability to prophesy. He gives someone else the ability to discern whether a message is from the Spirit of God or from another spirit. Still another person is given the ability to speak in unknown languages, while another is given the ability to interpret what is being said. It is the one and only Spirit who distributes all these gifts. He alone decides which gift each person should have" (1 Corinthians 12:7-11 NLT).

Question

What are some concrete things a young person can know about their identity with Christ that will keep them from being tricked?

Pastor Judy's response:

I just started with the basics. I went to the back of my Bible; I went to the index, and I looked for the word anger and I went to a verse that led me to that. And then I looked up the word 'fear' and searched for the verse(s) that was related to fear. That got me into the simplicity of it, familiar with a scripture a day. Whatever it is, you can go to the index of the Bible and look up what you are dealing with and there is a scripture for everything we are going through. That was so helpful for me as a young teenager.

Pastor Joey's response

I would partner that with a regular prayer life and everybody's prayer life is not created equal in the beginning. Prayer builds a relationship and intimacy with God whether you've been a believer (in Christ) for 10 minutes or you have been a believer for 10 years, or you are 16 now and you became a believer at 15, or you have been a believer since you came out of the womb because that's what your family does, is having regular conversations with God. It doesn't have to be these hour-long prayer meetings in the beginning. They just have to be moments where I'm talking to God regularly, where I'm telling Him what I'm thankful for, I'm telling Him who He is and what I believe about Him and then maybe I'm also praying for things that I struggle with that I might need help with. That communication solidifies your relationship with God and the more you talk to Him the more you feel close to Him.

Question

How can athletes stay connected to God with less time to attend church activities?

Pastor Judy's response:

The daily audio Bible. I played volleyball and softball; I'm such a sports person and I loved playing those things and sometimes I didn't necessarily have my physical Bible with me but it (audio Bible) would just read me the verse for the day. So, I was still getting my spirit fed somehow even without being able to attend church. We can have access to podcasts from any of our favorite preachers and teachers. There was a pastor I heard the other day say, "At the gym, I don't listen to music. I listen to the Word," so he's getting fed while he's working out his body.

Pastor Joey's response:

When working out or doing an activity that didn't require me to converse with anybody, I used to listen to a podcast. I tried to make sure it was spiritual in nature or leadership driven and that would feed me. Utilize the tools you have to embrace what you are trying to create in a culture of connection with God.

As a believer, you have to understand you're a son first. Your athletic ability does not determine your ability in God. When you understand your sonship, everything flows from that. Equally, invest as much as you're investing in your jump shot, in your right-handed left-handed layup, in your step-back drop-back spin around and shot (or skills from other sports); you have to invest in who you are as a son. That means pouring the Word and prayer and worship into you. Use worship as a weapon as you go through this walk because that's what's going to empower you by staying close to God. Your sonship will never be taken away. You can get injured and lose your career in a moment, but your sonship will never go away and that will take you into more rooms than even your athletic ability will.

> *Putting him (Jesus) first and all else will fall into place, aligns with "But seek ye first the kingdom of God, and his righteousness; and all these things shall be added unto you" (Matthew 6:33 KJV).*

> "But seek first the Kingdom of God and his righteousness, and
> all these things will be added to you"
> (Matthew 6:33 ESV).

Pastor Franklin Centeno
Maturin, Venezuela

Question

How can a young athlete who travels away from their church home and family for sport stay in tune with their walk with God?

Pastor Franklin's response:

Discipline. Spiritual life, just like sports, has its discipline. Physical exhaustion and fatigue can make searching for a church difficult in the first few days. However, maintaining your devotion, your studies of the Word, and your communication with your family can help in that first stage of training.

Question

With limited time to go to Bible study and in some cases fewer opportunities to go to church in person, what can an athlete do to not lose their Christianity?

Pastor Franklin's response:

Maintaining your devotion, your Word studies, and communication with your family can help in that first stage of training. However, looking for a church is a priority that cannot be left aside. Furthermore, once you have accepted Jesus Christ as your Lord and Savior, you are bought, and you are sealed by the Holy Spirit; there is no way you can undo that, as we read in Romans 8:31-39.

> "What shall we then say to these things? If God be for us, who can be against us? He that spared not his own Son, but delivered him up for us all, how shall he not with him also freely give us all things? Who shall lay anything to the charge of God's elect? It is God who justifies. Who is he that condemneth? It is Christ that died, yea rather, that is risen again, who is even at the right hand of God, who also maketh intercession for us. Who shall separate us from the love of Christ? shall tribulation, or distress, or persecution, or famine, or nakedness, or peril, or sword? As it is written, For thy sake we are killed all the day long, we are accounted as sheep for the slaughter. Nay, in all these things we are more than conquerors through him that loved us. For I am persuaded, that neither death, nor life, nor angels, nor principalities, nor powers, nor things present, nor things to come, Nor height, nor depth, nor any other creature, shall be able to separate us from the love of God, which is in Christ Jesus our Lord"
> (Romans 8:31-39 KJV).

Pastors Sean & Erica Moore
Phoenix, Arizona, USA

Question

What is the importance of knowing who you are in Christ?

Pastor Erica's response:

Knowing who you are is everything. When we don't know who we are, then we don't know how to behave, we don't know what to think, how to act, who to be around, what to do, and what not to do. Identity gives you boundaries for your entire life. When I know who I am in Christ, then it answers the question of, "What was I created to do?" The Bible tells us that we are created unto good works. Jesus told us that we are to imitate God like dear children.

> "For we are his workmanship, created in Christ Jesus unto good works, which God hath before ordained that we should walk in them" (Ephesians 2:10 KJV).

> "Imitate God, therefore in everything you do, because you are his dear children" (Ephesians 5:1 NLT).

Pastor Erica continues

When I (you) understand this, anything that doesn't look like God, I (you) should know it has nothing to do with me (you). It (Your identity) is going to let me know who I should be friends with, what I should be doing with my time, and what I shouldn't be doing with my time, what my focus should be, and what my focus should not be. It really governs every single decision I make. If I don't know that I am in Christ, if I don't know that God has a plan for me, that He loves me, that He's for me and not against me, if I don't know these things, then I might just do anything with my life. The Bible says, "Where there is no vision or clear direction, the people perish that cast-off restraint." When I know who I am and why I'm here, then I'm not going to waste my time with things that could be self-destructive or things that could destroy someone else's life.

> *"Where there is no vision, the people cast off restraint; But he that keepeth the law, happy is he" (Proverbs 29:18 ASV).*

Pastor Sean's response

One of the first things that we're given when we're born is an identity and one of the first things that we're given when we're born again (baptized) is an identity in Christ. Our identity is directly connected to who God is. God reveals Himself as a shepherd; therefore, it gives me an identity as a sheep. God reveals Himself as a king; therefore, it gives me an identity as a servant in His kingdom. He reveals Himself as a Father; therefore, it gives us an identity as sons and daughters of Christ. I think when we know who we are, there are certain things that we don't settle for anymore. When we don't know who we are, then I think purpose becomes unclear, vision becomes unclear, and the permissions we give to ourselves become unclear, but identity seems to settle all of that. As a pastor, because I know that I am a pastor, there are just certain things that I cannot permit myself to do and there are certain things that I do have permission to do because a part of who I am is to be a shepherd in God's flock.

Question

With an athlete's busy schedule preventing their regular attendance at church activities, how can they stay connected to God?

Pastor Sean's response

Hebrews tells us that the just shall live by faith.

> "Now the just shall live by faith; But if anyone draws back, My soul has no pleasure in him" (Hebrews 10:38 NKJV).

Pastor Sean continues

Instead of trying to go and practice our faith in a certain place, I think we just need to bring our faith into whatever environment we go into. Whether that's starting a Bible study with our teammates or wherever you go, wherever you visit just deciding to take the Word in you. And then be a model and an example. One of the admonishments (warnings) Paul gave to Timothy, who was his spiritual son in the gospel, is he (Paul) told him (Timothy), "Listen, don't let anyone despise your youth, but understand that when you're young you have a commission and a responsibility to be a model and an example in word, in conversation, in faith, and spirit in purity and love."

> "Let no one despise your youth, but be an example to the believers in word, in conduct, in love, in spirit, in faith, in purity" (1 Timothy 4:12 NKJV).

Pastor Sean continues

What I would encourage all young athletes to do is to first find out what God's Word says. And then number 2, implement those things into your life. And then number 3, find a way to bring the people in your circle into the faith just like you've made those decisions and commitment.

Pastor Erica's response

People need to take advantage of the time that they do have. You're traveling on a tour bus, you're on a plane... Put on your headphones, and put the Word in your ears. I listen to the audio Bible more than I physically read it. While you're listening, pause, and you can write a little note on your phone, and highlight it. Practice the presence of God, play worship music, saturate your environment, and create what you want. All of us can do that no matter how busy we are.

The Pastors' Take on Spiritual Gift Assessments

Pastor Shawn Scott
Clarksville, Tennessee, USA

Pastor Shawn informs

The growth track does spiritual assessments and personality assessments, but what I think is powerful with those spiritual assessments is that it goes through all the administrations of the gifts. You're answering based on what you know about yourself. What happens a lot of times is that people may have heard this language in one way but have never seen it broken into layers. Don't take it so far from where you think; I have the gift of a pastor that I need to have a church. You care for people, you want to see people's well-being, and you want to help them; that's the gift of pastoring. Just because you have this gift doesn't mean you have to function in the office and go start a church now.

When people don't understand their grace, they don't know how to handle it or steward it when these things start to happen. So, if they're hungry for money, now they're trying to use their gifts more to gain profit for themselves rather than build God's church. We take people through this process and allow them to function in different spaces in the church or organization. Now that they know this about themselves, these are the particular departments in which these gifts function. So now it makes sense; they are encouraged; they move in some sense of direction.

When a person doesn't know their spiritual gifts, they're thinking that it's them, not realizing that when you come into a relationship with God, God has given you something through the Spirit of God. If you don't have anybody that can help you understand what that is, you'll hijack that thing and take it somewhere else. A lot of people use their gift for personal profit, not realizing this is a gift God gave you to build His kingdom.

Pastor Christopher Deletsa
Lille, France

Please explain the differences of gifting and how a person can find their gifting.

Pastor Christopher's response

People focus too much on the gifting, to forget who (Jesus) is gifting them and what's the purpose of that gift. The Bible says, "The gifts of God is without repentance." God cannot take back His gifts, gifts He gives you. You have to know the reason of that gift.

> *"For the gifts and calling of God are without repentance"*
> *(Romans 11:29 KJV).*

Pastor Christopher Continues

The principal purpose of that gift is to propagate the kingdom of God. Establish His kingdom on the earth and be a witness to the people around you. Gifting doesn't mean that you can't propagate the gospel. Your gift needs to now be empowered by the Holy Spirit, that's why the apostles were with Jesus Christ more than ten years. He (Jesus) was teaching them, imparting them, giving them lessons, but he still told them to tarry (stay) in until they're endued with the Holy Ghost so that they can be a witness.

> *"And now I will send the Holy Spirit, just as my Father promised. But stay here in the city until the Holy Spirit comes and fills you with power from heaven" (Luke 24:49 NLT).*

Pastor Christopher Continues

Gifting doesn't make you a witness; it is the power of the Holy Spirit that comes upon you to be a witness. How then do you find out your gifts? I will use my experience as an example. At the age of 17 my dad told me, "You will be a doctor." But deep down I knew that's not my place, I hate to see blood, I hate to take medicine. One of the ways you can know what God has created you for is to know what are the things deep down you do easily without being told, you find passion in it. I have a lot of people around who come to talk to me, I assist people and I find joy in doing it. God is calling me. He allowed me to be in a leadership position, so I stood up to develop my leadership skills. And step by step God was taking me from that stage to university. God got me to lead people in the campus fellowship and then to where I am right now. We may deduce the plan of God (be careful not to do this), so always let the will of God take absolute (control).

Pastors Joey & Judy Salinas
Phoenix, Arizona, USA

Is there any way athletes can learn their gifting(s) earlier in life as athletes tend to leave home earlier than most people?

Pastor Joey's response

Pay attention to things that you already do well. Pay attention to when you know things that others don't know, when you perceive things that others don't perceive. When you realize it and recognize it, pray into it. As an example, if I (you) naturally were able to understand the Bible, I would read it, and it would become alive to me and I can make complex things simple, easier than the regular person quickly. And when I (you) notice that about myself (yourself), I pray into it. God, thank you for that gift. I thank Him for what I'm naturally gifted by Him to do. I ask God to allow me to own that craft better. So, you acknowledge it first, pray into it secondly, and you own it and practice it more often. That's how you get better at it.

For people in the midst of their gifting or who are not yet trained in their gifting, how can they not become overwhelmed?

Pastor Joey's response:

We have to know where the gifting comes from. It (Bible) says, "The gifts come from the Lord." Acknowledging that there is nothing that you could've done to make that gift happen, and there's also nothing you can do to make that gift go away, there's peace in the midst of that. So if you're involved in the middle of your career, in the middle of what you do, and you discover a gifting and it becomes burdensome, you become overwhelmed by it, instead of doing that say, "I didn't create this gift." It wasn't given by me, it was given by God, so because of that I'm giving it to Him. When you give the gift that God gave you back to Him, I'm not saying surrender (give it up) it, but instead saying God I'm approaching it with curiosity. I wonder what this (gift) is, I wonder how I can utilize this (gift) better, I wonder which ways I can utilize this (gift) in my current path. When we do that, there's a peace that surpasses all understanding that comes over us and the gift that we have becomes the gift that grows. Growing a gift happens in acknowledgement of the gift and knowing that God gave it to you so you should go back to Him to allow Him to strengthen it and make it better.

> *"Every good and perfect gift is from above, coming down from the Father of the heavenly lights, who does not change like shifting shadows" (James 1:17 NIV).*

Pastor Judy's response

Having sensitivity, the gift of discernment, being a feeler, seer, dreamer, having visions and what other people would describe as being an empath, that's more so me. I would carry what I was feeling, even if I wasn't originally feeling it. But if I go into a room and all of the sudden, oh my gosh my heart is heavy, oh my gosh my heart's pounding, I'm feeling scared and I wasn't feeling this before. Is there something wrong with me mentally? As I began to grow in God and get the proper resources to learn about the spiritual gifts, God was like, "Hey, you're picking up and discerning there's someone in here that came with an anxiety. So you're feeling this heaviness because they came in with that and I want you to release a prayer over them." I didn't have to lay hands on them for it to happen, I just declared, "God, your peace over their mind." At moments

I did feel like I was going crazy. I almost asked Him (God) to take the gifts away. He (God) doesn't give us a gift to burden us, but it's learning to work through it. He says, "Carry one another's burdens for you in this way you will fulfill the law of Christ." He tells us that in Galatians, but He doesn't say keep one another's burdens. So I'm going to carry it, I'm going to pray it, and I'm going to release, here you go, it's yours (God).

> **"Carry each other's burdens, and in this way you will fulfill the law of Christ" (Galatians 6:2 NIV).**

Pastors Sean & Erica Moore
Phoenix, Arizona, USA

Seeing as athletes tend to leave home earlier than most, is there a way to discover your gifting earlier?

| *Pastor Seans' response:*

I personally believe your calling involves **4 Ps; People, place, purpose and providence**. I believe that we all have a grace to reach a certain group of people, to do it in a particular place, and we need God's divine providence and we're all called for a specific purpose. We discover these strengths and these giftings many different ways. We discover it through vocation, I think we discover it through volunteerism, I think we discover it through the things that we can do, and the things that we can't do, the things that we're passionate about and the things we have no desire for at all whatsoever, through our successes and through our failures. Because athletes travel so much, I think if you can find a church and you can attend online it (helps). A lot of churches nowadays have volunteer opportunities that people can get involved with just online. There are a lot of options available today where you don't have to physically be in a building in order to have a sense of community.

Community is huge when it comes to being able to discover your giftings and discover what you're passionate about and having people that you're accountable to. You can join a church that's in a completely different state and every time you move you're still a part of that same exact church.

Pastor Erica's response:

If someone's trying to discover their gifts, writing in a journal is really good. Pay attention to your passions, what motivates you, what drives you, what angers you, what frustrates you, what gives you energy. A lot of those things point to your purpose. In school we used to always get in trouble for talking, but look at what we're called to do, we're called to talk. Talk to your older family members, "What was I like as a kid? What were my strengths? What were my weaknesses?" You'll find that people will be saying the same thing. It will point you to a direction of, "Oh, that must be what I'm really called to do." And ask God. I was nine years old and didn't know anything about passion, purpose, future... I looked in the mirror one day and I said, "Why am I here?" And God answered me and said, "You're going to marry a pastor," clear as day. I was nine years old, so I wasn't thinking about marrying anybody. **Ask God questions**, "Seek and you will find," the Bible says. We need to seek in His Word, but we also need to talk to Him, because he'll give us specific instructions that we won't find literally in the Bible.

> *"Ask and it will be given to you; seek and you will find; knock and the door will be opened to you" (Matthew 7:7 NIV).*

Pastor Erica continues:

You might have to take a course (class). I always knew that I was prophetic in nature, but I didn't know how to activate that gift. So I took a class on prophecy and spiritual gifts. If I didn't put myself out there and practice what I think I'm called to do, I would never develop that skill. If you read the story of Joseph and it (the Bible) talks about how he can interpret dreams and that leaps on the inside of you and you're like, "Man, I want to be able to interpret dreams!" Well, you know what? **Ask God**, "Hey, God, will you give me a dream tonight? I'm expecting dreams and matter of fact, can you help me to know what it means?" Put a notebook by your bed with a pen and expect to have a dream and expect to write it down and **pray over it** and expect God to tell you what it means. You have to step out just like in the natural. If you believe you're going to be an athlete, you have to go to practice, you have to try out for the team. Same thing spiritually.

Pastor Sean's response:

Think about life outside of sports. Most athletes have a very short career. Start to think about what does life look like if all of the sudden my athletic ability was stripped away. What could I do every day for free? What would I be passionate about doing for free for the rest of my life if I never got paid for it but I would take the time to develop the skill and the ability to really excel in that field? Think about it. If you had unlimited time, unlimited resources, unlimited opportunities what would you do for free for the rest of your life and spend the time becoming really good at? I think that tells us a lot about our purpose. The other side is what angers you? What makes you mad when you look out in the world? Is it homelessness? Is it human trafficking? What are the things that really burn you on the inside? It tells you something about why you're here on the earth. What needs do you see? When Jesus in Matthew chapter 9 looked out amongst the people, he said that they looked like sheep that didn't have a shepherd. It activated His purpose and He started teaching and delivering and ministering healing amongst the people.

> *"When he saw the crowds, he had compassion on them because they were confused and helpless, like sheep without a shepherd" (Matthew 9:36 NLT).*

How can a young person not get their gift for God hijacked?

> *Pastor Sean's response:*

If you really want to know why you're here, you have to return to your maker. Ultimately no one knows us the way that God does. Scripture tells us God knows our down sitting and our uprising. He knows our thoughts when they are far off, He understands our frame, He's well-appointed with all of our ways. There's no one on the planet that understands us the way that God does.

> *"You know when I sit and when I rise; you perceive my thoughts from afar" (Psalm 139:2 NIV).*

> *Pastor Sean continues:*

If you really want to know your purpose, then you can't leave it up to assessments and other things that we utilize to try to get to know ourselves. We can't leave it up to those things to reveal that stuff to us. I believe that ultimately God wants to reveal to us personally why He put us here on the earth. Our calling is oftentimes revealed in layers, we'll get a piece at a time. When a piece gets revealed and you're faithful in carrying it out, then God will reveal to you what that next piece is. But we have to make sure that in the world that we live in today that we are not turning to just any voice to speak clarity and order into our lives but that we're going back to the one (God) who made us to ask, "What did you have in mind when you created me?" Most times when it comes to our calling, we won't be the only one that knows. There will be other people around us in our circle who will also be aware of what it is that God has placed in our lives and in our hearts to affirm it, to confirm it, and to help assure us that we're on the right path, we're on the right course doing what we're supposed to be doing. I always say that if the only two eyes you have looking at you are your own, then you don't have enough people looking at you. Other people should be looking into your life and confirming and affirming what you already know in your heart.

Practical Guide for Growth

This workbook offers Christian athletes practical advice and thought-provoking questions to spark meaningful reflection. Addressing diverse challenges within their communities, it provides biblical wisdom and solutions. Each chapter ends with self-reflection prompts, enabling athletes to apply principles and foster personal growth. These questions encourage reflection, discussion, and application of chapter principles, aiding athletes in deepening their faith and navigating sports culture challenges.

These questions aim to encourage reflection, discussion, and application of the principles presented in each chapter, helping Christian athletes deepen their faith and navigate the challenges of sports culture.

Instructions

- Reflect on past experiences, both positive and negative, related to the chapter's topic.

- Explore your thinking and creative abilities, uncovering hidden tools within yourself.

- Analyze the effectiveness of different approaches and tools used in past scenarios.

- Write down your outcomes and identify the tools that helped you the most.

♦ If working alone, seek input from fellow believers to ensure a balanced perspective for group discussion questions. *"I encourage you to seek input from multiple people of faith to ensure a balanced perspective for group discussion questions."*

Knowing Who You Are in Christ

Question 1

Who are you in Christ?

_____

_____

_____

_____

_____

Question 2

Why is it important to know who we are in Christ?

_____

_____

_____

_____

_____

Question 3

What does knowing who you are in Christ allow you to do?

_____

_____

_____

_____

_____

Question 4

What is the five-fold ministry? Do you know your role in ministry?

_____

_____

_____

_____

_____

Question 5

How can you find your position in the five-fold ministry?

_____

_____

_____

_____

_____

_____

Question 6

Who can we contact spiritually and physically to gain insight to answer our questions about God's existence/decisions?

_____

_____

_____

_____

Question 7

Discuss some of God's promises. Which of God's promises are meaningful to you? Why?

_____

_____

_____

_____

Question 8

Explain the relationship of God the Father, God the Son (Jesus) and Holy Spirit.

_____

_____

_____

_____

_____

Question 9

What are good ways to keep growing in Christ with limited time for church activities?

_____

_____

_____

_____

_____

Question 10

What are the fruits of the spirit and how can a person find their gifting from God?

_____

_____

_____

_____

_____

_____

Question 11

What is the difference between gifts and anointing?

_____

_____

_____

_____

_____

Question 12

How can a person find their gift from God?

_____

_____

_____

_____

_____

Question 13

Does God take away our gifts?

_____

_____

_____

_____

_____

Question 14

Reflect on a time when knowing your identity in Christ helped you overcome a challenge in your athletic career.

_____

_____

_____

_____

_____

Question 15

How does knowing your identity in Christ influence the way you interact with teammates, coaches, and opponents?

_____

_____

_____

_____

_____

_____

Question 16

How does your identity in Christ shape your approach to competition and training as an athlete?

_____

_____

_____

_____

Question 17

In what ways can knowing who you are in Christ help you overcome challenges and setbacks in sports?

_____

_____

_____

_____

Question 18

The best place to learn about God is _____.

_____

_____

_____

_____

_____

2

Spiritual Protection

"

The 'full armor of God' consists of the helmet of salvation, the breastplate of righteousness, the belt of truth, the shoes of peace, the sword of the Spirit and the shield of faith, and prayer.

– Drake Reed

"

"Lord Jesus, thank you for giving every reader a complete understanding of their hedge of protection in you, in the name of Jesus. Amen."

Throughout life, no matter where a person is from, we all want to feel safe and secure. Most people do not want to be in the line of fire for anything unsettling or traumatic. But let me be very clear and upfront, you're a target in more ways than one. You're a Christian, which means your light is shining bright. You're also a highly coveted foreigner in your sport and will be a media headliner who is expected to be the best or one of the best players on your team if you are not playing in your home country.

Being a high-profile athlete brings responsibilities and pressures that most of us are used to after playing college sports. Still, playing out of state and internationally will be a bit different as your safety net of friends, family, and church home will not be present to shield you from those who may wish you harm. Prayer from those in your community at home can be easily forgotten over time, as the old saying "out of sight, out of mind" will become a reality, and what to pray for and against will be blurry for many folks at home as their understanding of the country and community you're going to live in will be limited. I will discuss territories in the next chapter to help you understand this more deeply. Jesus even warns his disciples of impending persecution:

> *"I am sending you out like sheep among wolves. Therefore, be as shrewd as snakes and as innocent as doves"*
> *(Matthew 10:16 NIV).*

Understand that you will not be visiting different states and countries to go on vacation; you're going to do a job. You will have plenty of fun, but with the job will come new challenges that most families are not accustomed to dealing with.

Statistics

Parents' Survey

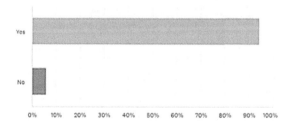

Do you pray for your child/children every day?

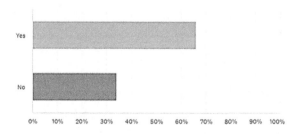

Does your child know what the armor of God is?

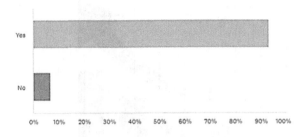

Does your child know how to pray?

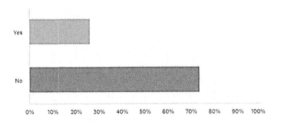

Does your child know what the five-fold ministry is?

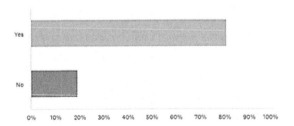

Is having a local church home out of state or abroad important?

The Pastors' Take on Parents Spiritually Protecting Athletes

Pastor Nathan Freind
Geelong, Australia

Question

How can parents spiritually protect their children when they're away for sports?

Pastor Nathan's response

Parents, your prayer life has to go to another level, too. Get your grandma, your aunties, your small group, and your church to pray for your kids because the world has a lot to offer and it can be a confronting place. Prayer is huge but I think you need that confidence in and trust from God that you've done a great job in raising your kids. You can't be too overprotective, checking on them every two minutes. You can certainly help by being an ear to listen to. On the practical side of things, do some research yourself. What churches are in the area or what connected groups are in the area that they can get in touch with? Do they have a Chaplain or a chapel at the university or the college (high school) that they're going to? Ultimately, as a parent, the hardest thing to do is to step back and allow them to find themselves (your kids) in their Christian walk. Ultimately, my Christian journey is not through my mum to God, it's me directly to God because we're always children (to our parents) at the end of the day. Sometimes, as parents, we play that middle person, without meaning to at times, and sometimes we have to move that middle place so they (your kids) can have that direct encounter with Him (God).

Pastor Jonel Marcelo
Malay, Aklan, Philippines

Question

How can a parent best spiritually protect their children?

Pastor Jonel's response

The best education comes from home. Let (teach) them more and be guided by the Holy Spirit. Educate your kids from God's Word at home. Like proverbs says, "Train up a child in the way he should go, and he will not depart from it."

> *"Train up a child in the way he should go: and when he is old, he will not depart from it" (Proverbs 22:6 KJV).*

Pastors Joey & Judy Salinas
Phoenix, Arizona, USA

Question

How can a parent spiritually protect their kid(s) when they're not around?

Pastor Joey's response

Parenting is all about contact, having contact, and creating moments with your kids. Some of the things I remember from both my daughter and my son are moments when I've had conversations with them about God. Your number 1 assignment is to make God a part of who you are as a parent. They (your kids) are going to get what you have and if your bar of living your Christian walk is down here, they're only going to get a little bit of what you have. You have to raise the bar spiritually on what you're going after yourself as a parent first. Secondly, you have to create contacts with your kids that talk about the things of God and pray with them. My wife intercedes for my kids. She would write prophecies for our kids in their bedrooms. It would be about their identity (with Christ) and who they are, and she would remind them of that prophecy about who they are regularly to the point that they did not doubt that God believed that about them regardless of what they had going on in their own life. Raise the bar with your walk with God, first. Secondly, talk about and create moments with your kids where you do the same. And lastly, you intercede like no one's business. You pray about the things they don't mention and then you mention things that you need to pray about.

Pastor Judy's response

There's a level of surrender that you have to have with God on a daily basis. "Hey, I'm not with my kids 24/7, but Lord, I'm trusting you with them."

God had walked me through, "Hey, you trust Me with everything else but your kids because you have these fears." (The fear is) I'll become the helicopter parent, like, God, I don't want them to get hurt, I don't want their hearts to be crushed, I don't want them to step out of Your will. Job had a repentance party before the Lord on behalf of his children even if he didn't know they were sinning or not. What I can do is cover them, encourage them and then, as they get older, our relationship goes from parenting to more coaching. I love you; I'm going to be there for you but I can't ground (punish) you anymore, I can't tell you what to do, but I'm still going to speak and prophesy the Word of God over your life. There are times when I've driven to where my child is and said, "Hey, God wants me to warn you about this, this, this…" And it ended up happening. Then there are times when God shows me something but He's like, "Be quiet, you're not allowed to say anything; you're only allowed to pray. I'm teaching them something." Parenting goes hand in hand with the Holy Spirit (Jesus) and asking Him for direction on the daily. There's nothing like just talking to God. Every child is different as well but trust, surrender, holding God's hand along through the process, and declaring what you see your child coming to be as an adult is just so powerful speaking life into them.

> "When these celebrations ended-sometimes after several days-Job would purify his children. He would get up early in the morning and offer a burnt offering for each of them. Job said to himself, 'Perhaps my children have sinned and cursed God in their hearts.' This was Job's regular practice" (Job 1:5 NLT).

Question

When a person's kid(s) is living in a country where Christianity is not commonplace, does the kid need more people praying than just the parent(s)?

Pastor Joey's response

Think about some of the words that were told specifically through God's Word to the disciples. He said, "Don't stop getting together." The gathering doesn't always need to be physical, but now in this world, gathering could mean one phone call away, one video meeting away, and one video chat away. You cannot stop gathering together because of the power of His Word. We utilize His Word to activate things in our life. The Word says, "If there are two or three in agreement upon anything on this earth, I am in the midst of it." There's power in numbers, that's why gathering is important. I need somebody to declare something and I need an amen from somebody else. That's why God uses the force of prayer and the force of gathering to interact together to create powerful moments.

> "Again, truly I tell you that if two of you on earth agree about anything they ask for, it will be done for them by my Father in heaven" (Matthew 18:19 NIV),

> "Don't stop meeting together with other believers, which some people have gotten into the habit of doing. Instead, encourage each other, especially as you see the day drawing near" (Hebrews 10:25-27 Common English Bible).

Pastor Erica Moore
Phoenix, Arizona, USA

Question

How can parents cover their kids spiritually once they've left home?

Pastor Erica's response

The best way we can protect our kids is with our words. We should be teaching them the Word of God and we should be reminding them what God says about them. "You can do all things through Christ who gives you strength. If God be for you, who can be against you?" Intimidation is going to try to come and psych them out. Okay, you got the contract you were believing in. But now you're out there and it's: "You're not smart enough for this, you're not old enough for this, you don't know what you're doing." All those voices of intimidation, some of them are internal, some of them are from the devil, and some people will be talking to them. They (your kid(s)) have to have enough Word (scripture) in them to combat that. So, we (parents) can give them scriptures, we can give them podcasts to listen to. We can record our voices and send it to them, encouraging them. We can constantly affirm them with our mouths and tell them, "Hey! I believe in you, but guess who believes in you even more? God does." That's HUGE! And just helping them to understand different pitfalls, maybe they don't understand the different religions in the town that they're going to, but you can look it up and share that information with your kids. Also, regarding prayer, I know the expression is, "All I can do is pray," but it's, "First, what I can do is pray" and then what else can I do? Because prayer is such a vital weapon. When we pray, we are coming against demons, principalities and those things that we don't know and we're attacking them where it matters; in the spirit realm because things happen in the spirit before we see it in the natural world. So, if you bind that demon that's trying to mess with your kid, it can't mess with your kid. I would pray and I would give them the Word. I think the best way to protect them is what we say with our mouths, what we say about them, and what we say directly to them.

Levels of Protection

Prepare yourself to explore various levels of protection, ranging from physical to spiritual, as we delve into strategies and practices to safeguard your well-being and success as a Christian athlete.

Baptism

There are several keys of protection for a Christian and the first is baptism. Accepting Jesus Christ as your Lord and Savior is very essential to being protected by the blood of Jesus. Many of us are not thoroughly aware of the importance of the blood of Jesus and why His blood is so vital to our safety. But in this particular chapter, we are going to focus on the blood of Jesus as protection. For a young Christian, what you need to understand is not just that Jesus died for our sins granting us eternal life (in heaven), but also that many places you travel to do not live by New Testament guidelines, meaning that they don't accept Jesus as being God. Many people know of Jesus and have heard of his greatness, but that doesn't mean they believe in Him as God, nor does it mean they're baptized. In any case, there are many verses in the Bible that talk of animal sacrifice to atone for sins, as well as many people into witchcraft, sorcery, magic, paganism, worship of other gods, etc. What you will come to find is that in your travels there are going to be many people you interact with daily that practice these spiritual systems; some believe they're good, some don't, but many people use different spiritual systems nonetheless and you need to be covered by the blood of Jesus to be protected from anyone who would seek to harm you by these practices.

Some people utilize blood sacrifices to harm people spiritually, mentally, and physically, but you need not worry, as Jesus' blood sacrifice overtakes all blood sacrifices as long as you've been baptized in the name of the Father (God), of the Son (Jesus), and of the Holy Spirit. If you're ever in doubt about someone taking spiritual action against you, don't hesitate to plead the blood of Jesus from the crown of your head to the soles of your feet, and be sure to let your pastor and prayer warriors know you are under attack right away. If your pastor is not experienced in spiritual warfare, then find a pastor who is, if ever you're under attack.

Armor of God

Another very important layer of protection is the complete armor of God. In Ephesians 6:10-18 NIV, the Apostle Paul speaks vividly of this when advising men and women of God:

> "And that about wraps it up. God is strong, and he wants you strong. So take everything the Master has set out for you, well-made weapons of the best materials. And put them to use so you will be able to stand up to everything the Devil throws your way. This is no weekend war that we'll walk away from and forget about in a couple of hours. This is for keeps, a life-or-death fight to the finish against the Devil and all his angels. Be prepared. You're up against far more than you can handle on your own. Take all the help you can get, every weapon God has issued, so that when it's all over but the shouting you'll still be on your feet. Truth, righteousness, peace, faith, and salvation are more than words. Learn how to apply them. You'll need them throughout your life. God's Word is an indispensable weapon. In the same way, prayer is essential in this ongoing

warfare. Pray hard and long. Pray for your brothers and sisters. Keep your eyes open. Keep each other's spirits up so that no one falls behind or drops out"
(Ephesians 6: 10-18MSG).

"Finally, be strong in the Lord and in his mighty power. Put on the full armor of God, so that you can take your stand against the devil's schemes. For our struggle is not against flesh and blood, but against the rulers, against the authorities, against the powers of this dark world and against the spiritual forces of evil in the heavenly realms. Therefore, put on the full armor of God, so that when the day of evil comes, you may be able to stand your ground, and after you have done everything, to stand. Stand firm then, with the belt of truth buckled around your waist, with the breastplate of righteousness in place, and with your feet fitted with the readiness that comes from the gospel of peace. In addition to all this, take up the shield of faith, with which you can extinguish all the flaming arrows of the evil one. Take the helmet of salvation and the sword of the Spirit, which is the Word of God. And pray in the Spirit on all occasions with all kinds of prayers and requests. With this in mind, be alert and always keep on praying for all the Lord's people" (Ephesians 6:10-18 NIV).

As a young person in life who probably is not so experienced in the understanding of how to make sense of what is conveyed in the Bible, I will help you break this down into manageable segments. The 'full armor of God' consists of the helmet of salvation, the breastplate of righteousness, the belt of truth, the shoes of peace, the sword of the spirit, the shield of faith and prayer.

♦ The 'Helmet of Salvation' means, as stated above, that you are baptized.

♦ The 'Breastplate of Righteousness' means you are living right, following God's word, forgiving people, forgiving yourself, repenting, and, to the best of your ability, living a Christian lifestyle as Jesus would have you.

♦ The 'Belt of Truth' means understanding the truth of God's Word and living it. The truth will set you free.

♦ The 'Shoes of Peace' refers to you having peace due to you being filled with the gospel of peace, aka the Bible. Knowing the Word of God (the Bible) for yourself will be vital to accomplishing more in life and overcoming enemy attacks. The Bible contains the Prince of Peace (Jesus Christ), who lives inside of you and is known as the Holy Spirit.

♦ The 'Sword of the Spirit' is the Word of God, which is the Bible. Understand that the Bible is not just a historical book with stories and scriptures; the Bible is a weapon that can be used to break strongholds (evil refuges), cast out demons, heal people, and claim territories. When the enemy comes against you, you must utilize the sword of the spirit to go on the offensive. Part of going on the offensive is also praying in the spirit (speaking in the tongues), as Apostle Paul mentions.

♦ And the 'Shield of Faith' is your belief in the Word of God, your belief in Jesus, in His blood, and your belief that Jesus, His Father, and the Holy Spirit are all true. If you do not truly believe that what is in the Bible is true, then you will have major challenges when true opposition comes against you. An example would be going to practice every day and doing all of the physical training and skill work to become a better player, only to get to the games and not believe in what your coaches and trainers taught you. Not believing will end in defeat. Enemies will prey on any weakness you have in your armor.

♦ Prayer is the final piece of the full armor of God. Pray about everything, your protection, health, family, finances, relationships, etc.

There are other parts of Ephesians 6:10-18 NIV, that I will break down when we get to the chapter on territories.

The Word of God

The Bible is your next armor of protection. Reading your Bible daily is like working out daily; it makes you better. In the beginning, you may not be very strong, fast, or have the skills, but with consistency, you will improve significantly in each area. As someone who is baptized, you are already filled with the Holy Spirit, but being filled with the Holy Spirit alone is not going to be as forceful against opposition if the Word of God is not in your lexicon (vocabulary). It is important to know the stories, the scenarios, and the truths of the Bible with accuracy because, at different times throughout your career and life, it will be necessary to speak these scriptures with authority to defeat or prevent opposition. Speaking the truth of the Bible to the opposition will dismantle them and render them useless in many cases. Consider speaking the Word of God with authority as a weapon of mass destruction against opposition.

> *"For the Word of God is alive and active. Sharper than any double-edged sword, it penetrates even to dividing soul and spirit, joints and marrow; it judges the thoughts and attitudes of the heart" (Hebrews 4:12 NIV).*

Now think about this scripture. The Word of God is alive and active, which means exactly what it states. This is not some old book that old folks talk about; this is a book that is very much alive (actively working). The Bible contains much power and will penetrate the mightiest of foes. If the word of God was dead, then the words would not work. As your journey continues, it is normal to have questions and concerns, just as Abraham did, just as Moses did, and so on. Pondering is a normal response in our human lives here on earth but as you believe in the Lord with all your heart, belief will turn into knowing as your experiences of victory upon victory for the Lord will expand.

Another bit of information a Christian needs to understand about foreign places is that access to information is much different. For example, in a large country like the USA, a person may never think of traveling out of state or across the country. Based on statistics from the US Census Bureau, 80% do not travel to live more than one hour and a half (100 miles) outside of their hometown, no matter where they live in the USA.

80%

From my experiences outside of the states, many countries are the size of a state, so the average person tends to know a bit more about what is happening in their communities than someone who lives in California watching the news about what is happening in Florida. (Hendren/Porter/Sprung-Keyser 2022.) I say all that because when it comes to spiritual matters, the average person in the USA tends to know very little. From my experience outside of the States, when spiritual matters arise, people outside of America tend to know a lot more than Americans. People in many countries outside of the USA deal with horrific spiritual encounters regularly and have ways of dealing with them, which may or may not be of God. None of this is meant to frighten anyone traveling abroad and does not mean that you will always be in crazy situations or that foreign people are all into occult dark arts because that is not the case. This is just to make you aware of your surroundings so you can make better decisions and not unknowingly get into dangerous situations.

Prayer Team

Moving on to the next area of protection, which is vital to your safety and growth, is a prayer team. There are many prayer groups and many of those groups are good, but for where you are going, many of your domestic prayer partners do not understand what you will be facing and it will be important for you to have an understanding of it along with your prayer team so that you all can effectively pray for one another. A prayer team needs to be made up of powerful Christians who are truly living righteously. Having a righteous prayer warrior is of great importance because you want to avoid receiving any negative spiritual attachments from anyone who will be praying for you. This is especially important when receiving prayer from someone who is praying for you consistently. For example, let's say someone asks for prayer for protection from a prayer warrior and this particular prayer warrior has a drinking habit. All of a sudden, after this person prays for you, over time, you have the urge to drink or you have the imagination of getting drunk. This is a basic way to understand the importance of having someone who is living righteously to pray for you.

Understand that sin opens doors that can invite unclean spirits. This is similar to inviting bad people into your home. If you're baptized, your body is the temple of the Holy Ghost, and it is your responsibility to keep your temple pure and not invite sin into your doorways (eyes, ears, nose, genitals, anus, etc.). These are the areas in which the enemy looks to influence and penetrate through various forms of influence, whether it be media, music, relationships, and so on. When someone prays for you, they are opening themselves up to being met with resistance from any unclean spirit that may be attached to or trying to attach to you. Also, when you receive prayer from someone, you're permitting them to intercede (battle) spiritually on your behalf, which can also open you up to whatever they may be dealing with. If someone ever mentions that they're not in a good place to pray for you, then let them be. Your prayer group needs to consist of powerful intercessors who pray for hours like it's easy and who are led by the Holy Spirit. They need to be people of great integrity and above reproach. Your pastor may or may not be the most powerful prayer warrior in your circle; the best intercessor could be your mother, father, cousin, etc., but you need their covering daily.

Where you're living and what you're experiencing will determine the level of intercessors you need because some intercessors are powerful enough to cover one person, dozens of people, or hundreds, or thousands of people. It just depends on their gift from God. Understand that you should have a team of prayer warriors with different skills and abilities, no different than having a diverse financial team. Some may be healers, others may be deliverers, some may be prophets, and so on. This team of prayer warriors needs to be powerful enough to handle whatever enemy is in front of them. You will know them by the fruits they bear and they will be the kind of people who are not surprised or rattled by anything you share with them. Keep this in mind:

> *"Be wary of false preachers who smile a lot, dripping with practiced sincerity. Chances are they are out to rip you off some way or other. Don't be impressed with charisma; look for character. Who preachers are is the main thing, not what they say. A genuine leader will never exploit your emotions or your pocketbook..." (Matthew 7:15-19 MSG).*

These prayer warriors of integrity will also not be charging you money.

> *"I am the good shepherd. The good shepherd sacrifices his life for the sheep. A hired hand will run when he sees a wolf coming. He will abandon the sheep because they don't belong to him and he isn't their shepherd. And so the wolf attacks them and scatters the flock. The hired hand runs away because he's working only for the money and doesn't really care about the sheep" (John 10:11-13 NLT).*

This is a powerful scripture that puts things into perspective. The hired hand is someone asking you for money in exchange for spiritual services, whether it be a psychic, empath, or even people in the church with spiritual gifts who may misuse their power and abilities for financial gain. This does not mean using your churches' or prayer teams' services without ever paying tithes or being nice to them either. It is of God to pay tithes and it is decent to be kind to your prayer team with gifts and such. Others can fool even an experienced Christian, because there are some people on this planet with incredible power, and they may acknowledge God the Father, Jesus, and the Holy Spirit but also serve other spirits. For example, in Numbers chapters 22 and 23, as Moses leads God's people through the wilderness, the king of Moab, Balak, sends a powerful spiritual man named Balaam to curse God's people. Now, Balaam also believes in God but he uses his power for profit and also serves other gods. Balaam even prays and inquires with God the Father on this matter, showing his connection to God. As we see, Balaam is offered a divination fee from Balak, as we see in Numbers 22:7:

> *"The elders of Moab and Midian left, taking with them the fee for divination. When they came to Balaam, they told him what Balak had said" (Numbers 22:7 NIV).*

As noted above from the New Testament in John 10:12, Jesus Himself warns of the 'hired hand.' As stated in Numbers 23:23 MSG:

> *"No magic spells can bind Jacob; no incantations can hold back Israel..." (Numbers 23:23 MSG).*

Here, God speaks through Balaam to Balak that His people cannot be harmed by divination, magic, or evil omens. Balaam was gifted in prophecy but allowed his gifts to be hijacked by the enemy. This is the cunningness of the enemy. There may be times when your enemies cannot harm you directly and may try to utilize spiritually gifted people to come against you, and many of those people know not to play with God and others will go against God whether they know God or not. Keep your armor strong and God will shield you. To improve the accuracy of who to pray for, ask the Holy Spirit to reveal to you who needs to be your prayer warriors, in the name of Jesus.

Another solid way to receive prayer and wisdom is to have family prayer meetings. This can happen weekly, biweekly or however often your family decides. Having prayer meetings through online apps is also a good way to get more families involved, as most families have members in different cities. Bringing everyone in your immediate and extended families into a family prayer group will do much to heal the entire family, pray off generational issues, and inform one another on how to be successful in various areas of concern. Family prayer groups can be a game changer for any family.

A bonus tip is that, if possible, it is important to know specifically what is in front of you when praying for success or protection, as this helps with accuracy. For example, if a person is sick and you pray for healing, it would be beneficial to know which sickness can be prayed for directly. For example, many prayer teams ask for a person's full name to focus on that person's spirit during prayer, as this eliminates other people with similar names. Now, do not be disillusioned to think that praying for a person's healing in a broad sense is ineffective because many times, intercessors will find areas that need to be healed when they're flowing in the spirit and focusing on an individual but identifying the areas of concern is helpful in prayer. A prayer team flows in the spirit and tends to see more than just the surface of what is happening. They may see or feel physical pain, have visions of a person's childhood trauma, and so on, and in many cases, they are powerful enough to cast off any demonic presence once they know the basis of the unclean spirit causing issues.

Church Home

Moving on through protection, the next area of need is a good home church. Your home church in the States is great for home, but you will need to the best of your ability to find a local church in the state/country you will be living in. This can be very challenging for those out of the country because many times you won't speak the language. In some cases they may not have a Christian church in the area, as many countries may not have a sizable number of Christians. Keep in contact with your home church in your hometown because they will cover you, but also look for a reputable church in your state/country of residence. I will discuss what to look for when choosing a foreign church:

1. The presence of the Holy Spirit is imminent. If there is no presence of the Holy Spirit, it means it's a no-fly zone (don't go). If you go into a place and people are not excited to praise and worship, if they're not filled with gratitude for what the Lord has done for them, then those would be easy indicators of the Holy Spirit not residing in a place. If people are in there praising with both hands up, speaking in tongues, falling to their knees, or in prostrate positions unashamedly, then these are good signs of the presence of the Holy Spirit.

2. Understand that there are myriads of denominations and cultures that you may not understand, along with other forms of people who believe in God differently than what you're accustomed to seeing. For example, I lived in Austria in my early 20s and Christmas was on two different days; one on the 25th of December and another on January 7. I was totally confused and asked why and I was told by people there that protestants and Catholics do things differently. I was right in the breadbasket of Martin Luther and the church versus the state scenario. But later after my retirement, an elder Austrian man explained to me that in Austria they celebrate December 6th, December 24th and January 6th during the Christmas season. December 6th commemorates Saint Nickolas, a famous Bishop who passed away on the 6th of December. December 24th is celebrated instead of the 25th because they're taught that Christ is born on the 24th. And January 6th represents the day the Magi found

baby Jesus to give Him gifts using the star of Bethlehem to locate Him. There are many countries where Catholicism dominates, Lutherans dominate, and places like Israel utilize the Torah written in Hebrew. Most international/overseas players move from country to country every year or two so this can be very confusing. Knowing that, you are looking for Christians who speak your language and preferably an in-person church because the community of worshippers is what will give you the best chance at growth and protection because a local church knows the territory you're in and what you will be battling with more than your church in your home country. Internet churches, although convenient, do not offer the same community benefits or understanding of your area. For example, if your home church is in the United States and you live in South America, your pastor and fellow church members probably have little knowledge about anywhere in South America outside of news stations. This can make you a sitting duck in various ways because you are living in a different spiritual territory with different spiritual opposition and little to no knowledge of the surroundings. The spiritual forces faced in one city can be different than in another city, let alone in another state or country. Having a local home church, no matter where you're living, is very beneficial as long as you're following the guidance of your Lord and Savior, Jesus Christ of Nazareth.

3. Be extremely careful in countries that are dominated by different spiritual practices. Listen, you're not a missionary, a soldier, or a politician; you're an athlete looking to make something of yourself in a place foreign to you. Sometimes you will play in regions where major religions outside of Christianity such as traditional religions, atheism, and so on, may dominate. There will also be undercurrents of occult practices. There are still plenty

of countries where Christians are not welcome and get persecuted (treated harshly), and you may not be exempted because you're an athlete. In some places, people will pressure you to convert; in other places, people will 'play' Jesus and add traditional beliefs or esoteric aspects to the religion. You will notice this in people wearing cult-like medallions, crystals, or clothes with unique symbols on them. Also, if many people are hesitant to shake hands, hug, or visit people's homes, many times it is because there may be people using dark arts in the area regularly. When in a country where there are very few to no Christians, it is best to stick with Internet churches and praise and worship at home.

4. Ask God for wisdom in choosing a church. Choosing a church in your hometown may be challenging, but choosing one abroad can be daunting. Do not be fooled into thinking that the above signs alone are 100% accurate, as you can find foul play in any place. The important thing to remember is why you're there and to let the Holy Spirit guide you. The church is here to teach us sound biblical doctrine so we can be grounded in our faith. A tree without roots can be blown over. We are in the world but not of it, and the church is important to keep us on the right track in God's will.

"Then we will no longer be immature like children. We won't be tossed and blown about by every wind of new teaching. We will not be influenced when people try to trick us with lies so cleverly, they sound like the truth" (Ephesians 4:14 NLT).

In the beginning, we are like toddlers in that we have less experience and knowledge about the Word of God and the world. Having a church home with knowledgeable and experienced teachers who accurately utilize and teach the Word of God is essential in our life's journey because, from time to time, challenges will arise along with life-changing decisions. It's important to be in a church where people know which scriptures and actions to take to unlock blessings, heal, and defeat the opposition, among other things.

> *"Be devoted to one another in love. Honor one another above yourselves" (Romans 12:10 NIV).*

Your church is a team game just like sports; even in individual sports like tennis, golf, and track, athletes still need a team of coaches, trainers, agents, and such. Based on God's Word, we must love and honor one another. A church without genuine love will cause harm to the people. Church hurt is real and it is important to understand that people in churches are still people who make bad decisions and mistakes like anyone else. Never forget your reason for being in your church because this will keep you in line if you do experience some unfortunate challenges with others. Be sure to forgive everyone and apologize to make peace and resolve conflicts.

> *"Be kind and be compassionate to one another, forgiving each other, just as in Christ God forgave you" (Ephesians 4:32 NIV).*

Most people come into the church under duress to be cleaned up, while others grew up in the church and had their transgressions exposed over the years, from childhood. The key is to be with good people who are working to get better and to help you on your walk with God. In Romans 12:9-13 NIV, Apostle Paul breaks our responsibilities to one another in the church down to sincere love and devotion, despising evil, honoring others more than yourself, sharing information from God to help others, being joyful, patient, and so on. In so many words, do your best for God and His people.

Personal Prayer

Personal prayer is also a staple of protection. Quoting scriptures daily, such as Psalms 23, 27, 91, and many other protective scriptures throughout the Bible, along with your prayers for traveling grace, healing, a hedge of protection, and so on throughout each day, is a solid layer of protection. It is important to always pray daily, even when you're fatigued, because this keeps the enemy at bay, knowing that you're a willing participant in your protection.

> *"Be cheerful no matter what; pray all the time; thank God no matter what happens. This is the way God wants you who belong to Christ Jesus to live"*
> *(1 Thessalonians 5:16-18 MSG).*

Many times, bad things happen and blessings aren't fulfilled due to lack of prayer. God's people and angels will work on your behalf, but it is your responsibility to tap into your own personal prayer life, as you have free will to choose. Remember to always end your prayers with "in the name of Jesus, Amen."

Forgiveness

Forgiveness is one of the most overlooked areas of protection. Most people don't view forgiveness as a method of protection. Having unforgiveness in your heart prevents blessings from manifesting in real-time. The blessings could be healing, financial promotions, relationships, prosperity, and many others. Let us take an example of a water faucet and a balloon. The faucet represents God; the water represents blessings, and the balloon represents unforgiveness. As a person's prayers to God prompt the Lord to turn on the water faucet of blessings, the blessings begin to flow toward the person. Unfortunately, being unforgiving has placed a balloon on the faucet, so now the balloon is being filled up, getting heavier and heavier. This balloon of unforgiveness is getting so heavy over the person's head that now it's affecting the person's speech, thought processes, and behavior. The balloon of unforgiveness is so big that it's starting to cover not only the person's head but other parts of their body. The unforgiving person is losing more and more opportunities every day, which makes the balloon stronger as the person has now developed hatred and rage. The unforgiving person knows that something is not right because they've been praying, they've been working out, and they've been giving their best effort. But this person must stop neglecting the nail in his/her hand, whose point is forgiveness and whose head is Jesus. Once the unforgiving person grabs that nail and pierces the balloon with forgiveness in the name of Jesus, the blessings will cover the person. Many people are walking around saved and otherwise with their souls free but their blessings are bound as their unforgiveness has laid siege to their blessings, leaving their prosperity unprotected.

> "In prayer there is a connection between what God does and what you do. You can't get forgiveness from God, for instance, without also forgiving others. If you refuse to do your part, you cut yourself off from God's part" (Matthew 6:14-15 MSG).

God is faithful and just to forgive us of our sins as long as we're not hypocrites by not forgiving others for their sins against us. I've prevented my blessings at times by being unforgiving and not realizing my frustration, which stopped people from helping me with certain projects. I heard a preacher once talk about how we cannot be hypocrites and want forgiveness by not forgiving others. This struck a chord within me. That day I called about five or six people that, at the time, I felt like I'd never speak to or speak positively of ever again in my life. I called them, forgave them all, and apologized for anything I had done to prompt them to take their actions. What it did was free us all and allow both sides to move on, as both sides were bound; one from being unforgiving and having bitterness and the other from not being forgiven and feeling shame. I went on a week of forgiving others that were on my heart and any time someone mentioned to me people talking badly about me and that I may have contributed to their harsh feelings about me, I called them up and said I was sorry for anything I had done that made them angry with me. Emotionally and spiritually, this broke down barriers I didn't know were there. All sorts of blessings came out of nowhere for months afterward. To God be the glory.

It is hard for many to forgive others. Years of abuse, violations, jealousy, hateful acts, and dastardly deeds can create a balloon of unforgiveness in anyone. As children of God, we have to be the bigger person, even when the violation is so evil that we may want revenge.

"Dear friends, never take revenge. Leave that to the righteous anger of God. For the Scriptures say, 'I will take revenge; I will pay them back,' says the Lord. Instead, 'If your enemies are hungry, feed them. If they are thirsty, give them something to drink. In doing this, you will heap burning coals of shame on their heads.' Don't let evil conquer you, but conquer evil by doing good" (Romans 12:19-21 NLT).

We must do our best to cast these burdens on God so He can deal with the baggage and leave us clean from taking retribution. Protect your blessings and your mind by casting your cares on the Lord and forgiving those who've caused harm. It is better to forgive someone than to lose years of blessings. Forgiving others and yourself also prevents a person from having to be delivered from unforgiving spirits later in life. It is a normal fleshly feeling to want harm to come to those who've done us wrong, but it is of God to let Jesus handle the situation, in the name of Jesus.

Renunciations

Another overlooked area that spiritually protects us is renouncing affiliations. It is one thing to be forgiven and repent of sins, meaning a person lets go of their pain (forgive) and turns from bad behavior (repent). It is altogether different to renounce a sin, group, or person. For example, a person can forgive a person for getting them hooked on drugs and not deal with the drug dealer anymore but look the dealer in the face and tell them, "I renounce you and everything I've done with you in the name of Jesus," is a crushing blow to an enemy because it spiritually severs the ties between the person and the group/person/ spirits involved in the sinful acts. Renouncing our sins daily closes the door on the enemy's entrance points. It is beneficial to renounce any sin a person has committed, both knowingly and unknowingly, to prevent a good portion of spiritual attacks, both subtle and forceful. Renouncing sins does not have to be public and it doesn't have to be deep.

A person can simply renounce having a lustful eye towards someone and this can eliminate a person's desire to undress another with their eyes, thus preventing situations in which they might seek to seduce another into sexual sin. As followers of Christ, we can renounce gossip, jealousy, anger, and so many others daily, and this will close the doors to the enemy and change our negative behaviors over time in the name of Jesus. As followers of Christ, we can renounce gossip, jealousy, anger, and so many others daily, and this will close the doors to the enemy and change our negative behaviors over time in the name of Jesus.

Speaking in Tongues

Lastly, another form of spiritual protection is speaking in the spirit (tongues). Although many believe this to be gibberish, out of date, and so on, the reality is that speaking in tongues is a gift from God that we can all do with prayer and practice.

> *"And these signs will accompany those who believe: In my name, they will drive out demons; they will speak in new tongues" (Mark 16:17 NIV).*

Jesus made it very clear that if we believe in Him, we will be able to drive out demons and speak in tongues in Jesus' name. The key is believing in Jesus and His promises, along with believing that you're capable of doing what Jesus has said you can do. For me, speaking in tongues feels like an eruption of words that comes out when there are simply no normal words that can convey what needs to be expressed. This can happen when praying intensely, during praise and worship, or if there is demonic activity around you that needs to be fought against. When facing spiritual confrontations, sometimes simple rebukes or spoken words in our native tongues aren't potent enough. In these moments, speaking in tongues elevates our spiritual defense to a higher plane, breaking through barriers and pushing back against adversarial forces more effectively. This divine language empowers us to dissolve snares and strongholds, offering protection to those for whom we pray. Speaking in tongues is not limited to just breaking yokes and strongholds; some interpret the tongues and can prophesy based on interpreting the tongues. Like anything, practice improves this ability and you will need to sharpen your speaking in the language of the Spirit to become better at it and more effective. Some people will say that speaking in tongues is demonic or think someone is possessed when doing this. After my travels throughout the world, some people who practice other spiritual systems speak in tongues, and those people are also powerful, but do not be fooled because anyone who is truly speaking in tongues with the powers Jesus has imparted to us is speaking in the name of Jesus and that person will be baptized and will live the life that Jesus has led us to do. When a man or woman of God is speaking in tongues, have no fear.

> *"For anyone who speaks in a tongue does not speak to people but to God. Indeed, no one understands them; they utter mysteries by the Spirit" (1 Corinthians 14:2 NIV).*

Speaking in tongues can indeed be a powerful spiritual practice that edifies believers. In certain contexts, such as confronting demonic forces, the manifestation of spiritual gifts, including speaking in tongues, can play a role in spiritual warfare. The authority and power of Jesus are central in such situations, and when invoked by a person of faith, it can lead to the expulsion of demonic influences. However, it's essential to approach such matters with discernment, prayer, and a deep understanding of biblical principles.

The Pastors' Take on Speaking in Tongues

Pastor Christopher Deletsa
Lille, France

Please explain the importance of speaking in tongues because many believe it is not of God or they're being influenced by evil forces when speaking in tongues.

Pastor Christopher's Response

I started speaking in tongues at a very young age, but at the time I didn't feel free speaking in tongues, I felt like I was dealing with forces (demons) in me. Some years later, I rededicated my life to Christ. And just after that we had a Holy Ghost baptism class and we talked about the Holy Spirit, they told us that anybody can receive (the gift of speaking in tongues), the only thing you will do is "just ask." Since then, up until now, I feel empowered and edified. Speaking in tongues doesn't make you a Christian, but it's a sign of being a Christian, it helps you. It's the language of the spirit (Holy Spirit). The Bible says when we pray we don't know how we should pray, what we ought to pray for. But the Holy Spirit makes an intercession for us, to help with our infirmity, because He (Jesus) knows the will (of God). When we don't pray according to His (God's) will, emotions, thoughts, destruction come inside. When you pray in the Holy Spirit, you may not understand what you are saying, but you are engaging the spirit of God to pray on your behalf, to intercede on your behalf, to help your infirmities. Like it or not, your words (normal words) may finish in 30 minutes, in 10 minutes your words may finish. What the Holy Spirit does is that when you engage Him (Jesus) in the language of the Spirit, He (Jesus) carries that language and intercedes for you with the Father on behalf of the saint. The Word of God carries it and makes it the will of God for you.

How then do you receive the gift of speaking in tongues?

1. You need to know that Jesus Christ is your baptizer. John the Baptist said, "He that will come after me will baptize you with the Holy Ghost and fire." Jesus Christ is the baptizer of the Holy Spirit.

> *"I baptize you with water for repentance. But after me comes one who is more powerful than I, whose sandals I am not worthy to carry. He will baptize you with the Holy Spirit and fire" (Matthew 3: 11 NIV).*

2. You need to ask Him (Jesus). I want to speak in tongues, it's a gift He (Jesus) can give to you.

3. Start speaking, He (Jesus) gives you an utterance. Don't wait to start shaking, don't wait to start vibrating.

Pastor Christopher continues

If you read Jude chapter 1 verse 20 says, "Build yourself up in your faith." You need to build it up. Start a small build, and the Holy Spirit will help you in your utterance. If you're not speaking in tongues, it doesn't mean you don't have the Holy Spirit. The Holy Spirit comes on you as soon as you give your life to Christ because the Holy Spirit is the spirit of God inside of you. Speaking in tongues gives expression to Him (Holy Spirit).

> *"But you, dear friends, must build each other up in your most holy faith, pray in the power of the Holy Spirit"*
> *(Jude 1:20 NLT).*

The enemy is a copycat and can present itself as authentic when speaking in tongues.

Pastor Christopher continues

That's why I used my story (of speaking in the tongues before baptism and after baptism). Everything authentic has a copycat. What the devil tries to do is to copy God. He (Satan) will present it very well. Speaking in tongues doesn't make you a Christian, it's the fruit of the Spirit. We have Holy Ghost speaking Christians but they're not living the life of Christ, they're not expressing the fruit of the Spirit. The Holy Spirit doesn't speak in tongues for us, we speak in tongues not the Holy Spirit. We need to speak in tongues for the Holy Spirit to now give expression and carry it to God. People want the Holy Spirit to speak in tongues for them. That's why people don't have the gift of speaking in tongues, they feel like it's the Holy Spirit that needs to come and speak in tongues. No, it is you that needs to pray in tongues. The Holy Spirit is already inside of you (if you're baptized), you just need to exercise it. When you start speaking in tongues, you will know the beauty of it. I've never met anyone speaking in tongues that regrets speaking in tongues.

Practical Guide for Growth

This workbook offers Christian athletes practical advice and thought-provoking questions to spark meaningful reflection. Addressing diverse challenges within their communities provides biblical wisdom and solutions. Each chapter ends with self-reflection prompts, enabling athletes to apply principles and foster personal growth. These questions encourage reflection, discussion, and application of chapter principles, aiding athletes in deepening their faith and navigating sports culture challenges.

Spiritual Protection

Question 1

What are the layers of spiritual protection for Christians? Which layers are you currently using? Which areas do you need development in?

_____

_____

_____

_____

_____

Question 2

Explain the complete armor of God and its purposes.

_____

_____

_____

_____

_____

Question 3

What spiritual practices or disciplines do you incorporate into your athletic routine for spiritual protection?

_____

_____

_____

_____

Question 4

Describe a situation where you felt spiritually vulnerable as an athlete and how you sought protection.

_____

_____

_____

_____

_____

Question 5

How can you encourage and support fellow Christian athletes in maintaining spiritual protection amidst the challenges of sports culture?

_____

_____

_____

_____

Question 6

Describe a time when you felt spiritually vulnerable in your athletic journey. What steps did you take to protect yourself spiritually?

_____

_____

_____

_____

Question 7

How do you maintain spiritual discipline and connection with God amidst the demands of sports training and competition?

_____

_____

_____

_____

_____

Question 8

Share a personal experience where spiritual protection played a significant role in your athletic performance or decision-making.

_____

_____

_____

_____

_____

Question 9

How can we forgive someone who has done us wrong when we struggle to confront them? (Discussion)

_____

_____

_____

_____

_____

_____

Question 10

How can we forgive ourselves when we've made bad choices?
(Discussion)

_____

_____

_____

_____

_____

Question 11

When is the best time to forgive and renounce?

_____

_____

_____

_____

_____

Question 12

What has God's word done for you protection-wise? (Discussion)

_____

_____

_____

_____

_____

Question 13

Who should be on your prayer team?

_____

_____

_____

_____

_____

Question 14

Who are those you do not allow to pray for you? Why?

_____

_____

_____

Question 15

What is the significance of Baptism?

Question 16

How can parents spiritually protect their kids?

3

Territories

"

Make no mistake about this; there is no replacement for the Word of God.

– Drake Reed

"

"Father God, thank you for preparing us all for our journeys throughout this planet. Give us insight, wisdom, and the gumption to make decisions in line with your Word and for our safety and well-being, in the name of Jesus. Amen."

Locations of Pastors Who Provided Quotes

Spiritual

This section on spiritual territories will be eye-opening because this information, though talked about in a broad sense, is not typically known to most people. All people will experience the influence of territories no matter where they live, whether it be entering a different neighborhood, city, state, or country. If anything is unsettling in this chapter, understand that we will have to deal with all of these at some point especially if traveling domestically and abroad is commonplace in your life. Quite frankly, most people are experiencing the influence of territories without realizing it in their hometown. Have you ever landed somewhere on a plane or traveled in a car or train somewhere and your head began to hurt from pressure, had strange thoughts or visions, or began to be sick out of nowhere? This may be because your anointing is not wanted in the area due to entering a territory that is not under the direction of Jesus Christ of Nazareth. I say the name Jesus Christ of Nazareth because, as we travel and enter different territories, it is possible to meet people, whether they are in church or not, who have various spellings and interpretations of who Jesus is. Also, some people utilize portions of the Bible and will mix scriptures with other belief systems and put Jesus' name on top of them. Some imposters will try to sound as if the name they're speaking of is Jesus but they're copycats, no different than someone trying to look like a superstar by dressing and acting like them. If anyone ever prays for you, it needs to always be in the name of Jesus, referring to Jesus Christ of Nazareth. Understand that the world is much bigger and older than we will ever know and many people have the name Jesus even now. In other places, there are more people called Christ but you need to know you are calling on Jesus Christ of Nazareth when you are praying and praising because Jesus is no copycat. He is no mere human; He is the son of God. For a young, impressionable mind in their teens, 20s, or even 30s traveling the world, this can all be confusing, especially with easy access to the internet and algorithms that give us more of what we click on.

Every country on the planet has a spiritual belief system that dominates the land, whether it be Christianity, Islam, eastern religions, traditional religions, dark religions, and so on. I will not give the names of dark religions or other gods, as there are many and it is best not to invoke them by saying their names casually. Calling on other spirits, chanting, or thinking about them for extended periods can invoke an unclean spirit to approach a person. In Exodus 23:13 NLT, God the Father is speaking to Moses and tells him:

> *"Pay close attention to all my instructions. You must not call on the name of any other gods. Do not even speak their names"*
> *(Exodus 23:13 NLT).*

In the book of Joshua, we see how when Joshua grew old after his conquests of the promised land and allotments of the promised land to the 12 tribes, he warned the people of God about dealing with other gods. This was an interesting time as God's people conquered and, for the most part, destroyed the people who lived in the promised land to remove the worshiping of other gods and idols that were common in the land. The Lord knew if the spiritual territory was not defeated in the minds of the Israelites, then His people (Israelites) would soon turn away from God and be in trouble again.

> "Make sure you do not associate with the other people still remaining in the land. Do not even mention the names of their gods, much less swear by them or serve them or worship them. Rather, cling tightly to the Lord your God as you have done until now" (Joshua 23:7-8 NLT).

Right now, we follow the new covenant under Jesus as we are now filled with the Holy Spirit, but in many places, if you visit and live outside of your hometown, you may find a larger portion of people who live under the Old Testament mindset. Whether they believe in God the Father or follow another religion, you may see and hear many conversations, movies, TV shows, music, paintings, tattoos, and so on of people who worship other deities and spirits. Many will wear and pray over crystals, medallions, jujus, and other sorts of protective and healing devices. Many belief systems may confuse a person because if they read the Old Testament exclusively, it can open the door to believe other systems are the same but with different names. If you read through the Old Testament, you will see how even the priests had garments laced with all sorts of crystals and gems. In Exodus chapter 28, God gave Moses meticulous instructions on how to dress Aaron and his sons, who were to be priests. These instructions included everything from numbers which represented names and tribes, to colors, and to objects that appear to help with keeping a connection to God.

> *"And thou shalt make the breastplate of judgment..."*
> *(Exodus 28:15 KJV).*

> *"and onyx stones and other gems to be mounted on the ephod*
> *and breastpiece" (Exodus 25:7 NIV).*

These were items placed on the priests' chests. There are many other crystals and gemstones mentioned in Exodus that were part of the priestly garments, such as lapis lazuli, emerald, sapphire, amethyst, agate, and so on. What some people may do to inexperienced Christians is to quote the spiritual qualities of these natural objects, along with herbs, incense, and so on, and compare them to biblical stories such as Exodus. It is possible to be told things like, "See, it's even in the Bible," or "That book (the Bible) is to control people; they just don't want you to know you can do this yourself with the knowledge of nature."

Understand that without calling on God, our God-given gifts still work. But those gifts are limited without a true relationship with Jesus. Every knee has to bow to Jesus and every tongue must confess that Jesus is the Lord; that's just the way it is. Also, understand that enemies can be powerful and cunning (trickery) and will mix lies with the truth to gain your trust in them to take advantage of you. Remember, Pharaoh's magicians had staffs that could turn into snakes, just like Aaron's staff, which was empowered by God, but Aaron's staff swallowed their staff. God is more powerful than your enemies. Make no mistake about this; there is no replacement for the Word of God. Many other books and stories are very powerful, but the missing link is Jesus Christ of Nazareth because His blood sacrifice overtook all others and His Father created all there is, will be, and ever was. The more of the Word a person knows, the more battles they will win but the less a person knows, the more they're prey for their enemies.

While traveling, we can also hear and face new-age belief systems, which have some power but are mere pieces of what God has gifted us with. Many will say things like, "I don't believe in religion" or "I'm spiritual, not religious." Many like these are good people and work to be better every day. I was once one of them, but this is typically someone who has not been introduced to Jesus at all, properly or does not have legit experiences of utilizing God's promises to us. There are principles of nature, attraction, intention, and so on, which are offshoots of the biblical text, which will work a bit, but if you want to put it to the 'text,' use Habakkuk 2:2 and other scriptures on your vision board and see how much more a man or woman of God will accomplish with scriptures backing your goals as compared to not utilizing the word of God with your vision board.

All the above are basic things that can affect a Christian negatively. The opposition's tactics haven't changed; there is just different technology. But let's get a little deeper into these spiritual territories. The above paragraphs break down basic confusions that anyone can encounter no matter where they live, but the bigger challenge we will face is the demonic presence from a territory. The first sentence of Revelation 12:4 NIV sheds light on the opposition.

> *"Its tail swept a third of the stars out of the sky and flung them to the earth. The dragon stood in front of the woman who was about to give birth, so that it might devour her child the moment he was born" (Revelation 12:4 NIV).*

This scripture speaks of the devil taking one-third of the angels to earth with him. The stars (angels) who fell with the devil are called 'fallen angels' by many and are considered the demons and/or deities that we wrestle with today. The only one who knows the age of this planet is God, who created it. With that being said, the Bible only covers a couple thousand pages of what has happened on Earth, and it focuses on the Middle East, parts of Europe, and parts of Africa. There are many other places, such as Australia, North America, South America, Antarctica, East Asia, and so on, that have no stories in the Bible, so you must understand that there will be different sorts of enemies and stories in different places.

> *"For we wrestle not against flesh and blood, but against principalities, against powers, against the rulers of the darkness of this world, against spiritual wickedness in high places" (Ephesians 6:12 KJV).*

Anytime you move to another city, state, or country, you can expect to deal with different principalities and powers, aka demons, sins, etc., of different levels. They will come in different forms; some in the air, some in the water, some in the earth, some in the media, and so on. Some will try to visit your dreams and visions; others will entice lustful people towards you; and others will invade the media airwaves through your television, the internet, and so on. Many can be invited by you due to a lack of knowledge, a lack of action, a lack of awareness, a lack of discipline, or a combination of those. Lack of knowledge could mean a person doesn't know Jesus, hasn't been baptized, has low-level teachers, or doesn't know how to utilize the Word of God. Lack of action means that when someone knows something isn't right, they continue to put themselves in harm's way. Not rebuking the enemy, not reading the Bible, and not praying are all costly decisions. Lack of discipline can mean sharing too much private information, gossiping, skipping church and Bible study, not forgiving, or repenting.

Understand and know that, as a baptized Christian, your light shines in the spiritual world, whether it be the spiritual world in the physical realm or the spiritual realm when you're asleep. The spiritual realm exists when we're awake and asleep. A person's mind is typically focused on the physical world more than the spiritual, while awake people are busy with daily errands. Many people on the planet do have spiritual abilities and flow in the spiritual realm while awake as well. The more a person is in tune with seeing, hearing, and/or smelling spiritual entities, the more those spirits will want that person's attention. Like people, spirits have an agenda whether it be gaining someone's attention, wanting a favor done, or attacking a person based on their gifting. The enemy will never know your God-given assignment but the enemy can see your light and will seek to stop or convert you. As you're traveling through places, especially if it's an extended period, any spirit that is not of God may try to attack you. The stronger your gifting, the stronger the opposition, the stronger your armor, the stronger your opponents. Have no fear because, with the authority given to us, in the name of Jesus, there is nothing you cannot defeat. Unclean spirits can look as beautiful as the best-looking supermodel or as ugly as the worst horror film monster. The key is in knowing the word of God, having a man or woman of God mentor who understands these matters, and utilizing your authority when necessary. A person will need to have some insight from a prophet, apostle, or someone in the church with the ability to see, hear, and smell spirits; someone who has integrity and can guide in these matters of troubles with spiritual attacks. Christians have been given the power to rebuke and cast out demons. This also includes the power to not be touched.

> *"A thousand shall fall at thy side, and ten thousand at thy right hand, but it shall not come nigh thee"*
> *(Psalm 91:7 KJV).*

I remember at age 20, during my junior year in college, I faced a lot of stress and had a lot of failures that year. During my senior year, I wrote Psalm 91 on my sneakers and it felt as if a forcefield was around me at all times, like nothing could touch me, no matter how vile it was. I did not know that scriptures held such a high level of power at that time. There have been many times in my life when death seemed imminent, even times when my faith was low or nonexistent but God saved me every time. When I was in high school, there were many times I dealt with sleep paralysis; however when a pastor instructed me to say Psalm 91 every time I woke up and before I went to bed, in my dreams I would see the spirits around me, but they couldn't touch me. I would see the reward of the wicked but not be touched. Many times, after reading the Bible before bed, I would find myself rebuking and casting out unclean spirits in my dreams. The Bible is alive, meaning it actively works, and you must use it efficiently in all territories, both foreign and domestic. In many areas, there were wars, enslavements, spells, words spoken on a family or place, etc. As someone new to the area, how could a person know or understand these things?

For baptized believers of Jesus Christ, the Holy Spirit inside of us knows exactly what is going on and will guide us (when we ask for guidance) on what we need to pray on, what words to say in authority, how to bless our homes and other things that we need. Understand and know that free will is in play and we have to take actions along with prayers to see things come to pass. What you need to know is that you have the authority to defeat all enemies using the word of God. The scriptures have immense power to cast out and resist any demonic entity as well as remove spirits from hindering your blessings. But the scriptures themselves, although powerful, have to be put into action by you, with your own free will. Decree and declare the peace of God upon arriving at a place, and bless your home with holy oil prepared by a trusted pastor. The pastor who blesses your holy oil needs to be a person who is truly living righteously because you do not want any negative attachments from the person who blesses the oil. Have NO FEAR at all if you feel, see, or smell an unclean spirit. If a spirit comes at you while you're passing through somewhere, rebuke it in the name of Jesus. You only have to cast a spirit out if it is on you or if the Holy Spirit has permitted you to cast a spirit off of someone else. There may be times you may experience pressures on your head or other strange happenings when visiting places, this can sometimes be due to spiritual resistance in the area that sees your light shining and wants you to leave the area or to gain entry through your gateways (eyes, ears, nose, mouth, genitals). Prophets and Apostles tend to deal with more principalities and powers than those who are not because God blesses them with enough power to kick principalities and powers off territories. Unexplained or bizarre headaches, illnesses, job losses, and other unexplainable situations can be signs of spiritual opposition. Many people have been to places where the majority of the citizens act very differently and the energy is off in places with extreme poverty or famine, or places where there are occult symbols everywhere. These are signs of being in a different spiritual territory and a Christian may be subject to persecution of some level or unseen spiritual attacks.

Lastly, for the spiritual territories section, let me explain the heavens. Many times, people hear people say Heaven and heavens interchangeably and the Bible has sections using both singular and plural as well. In Christianity, we know there are three heavens; the first is the earth's atmosphere; the second is outer space, and the third is the heavens where God resides. The 3rd heaven is beyond the stars where God lives. The 1st heaven is the atmosphere above us. But the area that many people don't readily know about is the 2nd heaven, being space. Space is the 2nd heaven where major spiritual warfare takes place. One of the enemies' objectives is to block our communication with God. We pray and fast to get answers from God Almighty, but the enemy does his best to intercept the messages and blessings in the 2nd heaven. Think of prayer and blessings as a tennis match; we pray to God and the ball has to get past the net (2nd heaven) to God for God to send the ball back over the net to us. This is a constant communication with us. Many times, when prayers are not answered, it is because we need to fast to gain more spiritual power to push the prayers and receive the answers more easily through the heavens. The best description I can think of to explain how the heavens work is in the book of Daniel. Daniel fasted for 21 days as he wanted an answer from God and after 21 days an angel appeared to him.

> *"Then he said, 'Don't be afraid, Daniel. Since the first day you began to pray for understanding and to humble yourself before your God, your request has been heard in heaven. I have come in answer to your prayer. But for twenty-one days the spirit prince of the kingdom of Persia blocked my way. Then Michael, one of the archangels, came to help me, and I left him there with the spirit prince of the kingdom of Persia. Now I am here to explain what will happen to your people in the future, for this vision concerns a time yet to come'" (Daniel 10:12-14 NLT).*

Here, we see that Daniel's prayer request to God for understanding was immediately granted but Daniel's message was being blocked by the enemy. In this case, the one blocking the message was the 'Prince of Persia' which appears to be a spirit assigned to the Persian territory or a spiritual guru, invoking a spirit in the 2nd heaven to block blessings. This put the messenger angel of God in a position to have to spend time fighting to get to Daniel in the 2nd heaven instead of going directly to Daniel without hindrance. God hears us immediately and will grant our requests in the name of Jesus, but sometimes delays happen due to the opposition in the 2nd heaven before it reaches our atmosphere in the 1st heaven. The Apostle Paul speaks of this battle:

> *"For we are not fighting against flesh-and-blood enemies, but against evil rulers and authorities of the unseen world, against mighty powers in this dark world, and against evil spirits in the heavenly places" (Ephesians 6:12 NLT).*

Here, Apostle Paul mentioned 'evil spirits in heavenly places.' He was referring to the evil spirits in the 2nd heaven. In Ephesians 2:2 NIV, Apostle Paul referred to the devil as the ruler of the kingdom of the air.

> *"In which you used to live when you followed the ways of this world and of the ruler of the kingdom of the air, the spirit who is now at work in those who are disobedient"*
> *(Ephesians 2:2 NIV).*

This, again, refers to the sky space, and the airways. These are the spiritual territories; the earth's atmosphere (1st heaven), space (2nd heaven), and heaven (God's home).

Political Territories

Moving on from spiritual territories, let us talk about political territories. I remember when I was in Dallas, Texas, in my mid-20s doing my off-season workouts. I used to go to this barbershop and get my haircut by an old school brother. President Obama was running for office and everyone at that barbershop was talking about the political issues at the time. Each person voiced their opinions and when it was my barber's turn to speak, he said something I will never forget that put my life as a ball player in perspective. He said, "Young brother, the older I get, the more I understand there are two things that run this game... Politics and politricks." This is one area where most people get lost, not only abroad but in their own countries. In America, we get confused about our democracy, how it works, which party does what, and the like. Parties can be altered by certain candidates' views and the masses will never know the entire truth, along with many of the people in politics. The main thing we need to understand when playing professionally abroad is you're not in American democracy, you are not in the land of the brave or the home of the free. The country you are residing in has its own rich history, and heroes, and most people you meet couldn't care less about foreign political views in your country. Also, know that many people amongst you do not like the USA (or your home country, if outside of the USA) for one reason or another, whether it be they don't like our politicians, our policies, or our tourists. They may have bad relationships with your home country due to wars, trades, or a litany of issues that you typically will know little to nothing about.

Depending on the country you're moving to, your home country may even be a sworn enemy so walking around with open pride about your country or its movements can put you in imminent danger amongst local people who may or may not be affiliated with your team. Do not be foolish and attach yourself to movements in other countries because chances are you probably do not fully understand what is going on seeing as you're a foreigner with little experience in that country and you do not want to be placed on a no-fly list back to your home country. As a college or pro athlete, meeting mayors, governors, presidents, and royal families is common and it is possible for a politician to have a stake in the teams you play for or they go to the games for enjoyment no different than any other fan. Many politicians are very nice and respectable people just like in your home country. However, if you happen to be playing in a country that is not friendly to your home country, then be aware of whom you converse with and take photos with because you are not a native in that nation and you never want to put yourself in harm's way on political issues. Always remember when you're working in a foreign place to do your job. You're not there to play politics and how you think based on your own culture has little to no merits on what happens in the country you're playing in at large.

Continuing with political territories, let's break down the various political systems a person may be subject to living abroad. One is the monarchy, which is composed of royal families. This means the king, queen, and royal family run the entire country, make all of the rules, and dictate what happens. Also, an athlete may play in some nations that have royal families inside of the nation that is governed nationally by a republic or democracy, etc. Still, these royal families have a heavy influence on what happens because their families controlled the nation before they were colonized or before the country was forced to change their politics through war, unrest, or other reasons. It is possible to live with positions like prime ministers in countries with constitutional monarchies such as Australia. Prime ministers can also be positions in republics like France. The title 'Prime Minister' means something different depending on the political system as the prime minister can serve a royal family or a prime minister can be a president of sorts. Many countries may be republics in which the power rests with the people. If you're an American, this can sound very familiar, but many times these governments do not function entirely like what we're used to. Some countries are oligarchies, meaning a small group runs the country. Others have various forms of government such as socialism, which changed to communism as socialism is economical, etc., but as a foreign athlete, all you need to do is behave yourself. You will find the majority of nations across this planet are built on strong ethics and ideals of respect. We do not have to agree with everyone's politics or way of life, but do not disrespect people with self-righteousness. From my experience, people have the same political arguments and conspiracies in every nation on the planet, so don't be surprised by it. Just pay attention to what is being said to know if it pertains to your well-being and livelihood.

There are so many political issues going on in foreign countries that a person will not understand due to their lack of information, lack of language knowledge, or lack of cultural knowledge. I remember living in Australia at age 23; seeing the world news didn't feel the same as watching the news in the States. The news in Australia showed political issues in

China, Europe, and various nations bordering the Indian Ocean. I remember there was a news story in Greece where there was a protest by tens of thousands of people outside of parliament. I was totally confused because at that time, being just 23, I had never seen people in front of a capital building protesting that angrily. Later that year, I was playing in France and my coach informed us we had practice at 10:00 a.m. I drove to practice and there were hundreds of people on the streets; I thought there was a parade. Then I took another street and thousands of angry people were at the top of their voices. I was worried about being late to practice because being late to practice is never good. The people in France were angry about social security being pushed back and I, being a newcomer who couldn't speak French at the time, had no clue as to the political issues in the country. I was just headed to practice and nearly got caught up in all the drama. It was a bit scary because I didn't understand the language or what was going on and I was fresh on the team, so I didn't know if I'd be penalized for being late. No one cutting off the streets looked like me so I thought maybe I'd be harmed because I'm black; it was troubling. Years later, at age 26, I was in Libya playing and this country had some of the nicest people I've ever met but they were in a state of political unrest. There was no one in charge of the government at the time. Here I was just going to play ball, not having an understanding of what was going on, and having been the first person in my family to travel abroad at such a high rate, no one could talk me out of it and others whom I knew didn't understand the ramifications of it either. Unfortunately, I found out the hard way. In Libya, Islam is law and I had no understanding of this. It was confusing because religion was mixed with politics and I didn't understand Islam or their politics. Meanwhile, I was just working to be a great player in their league. That year, I found out that protests are not always peaceful, they can be very deadly. We had a road game canceled due to a protest, a home game canceled due to a battle in the city we were supposed to travel to, and all sorts of frightening things happened due to civil unrest. My entire experience there was eye-opening, to say the least. It took years for me to make sense of my time there but what I can say to it is to follow what the Word of God says.

I made an idol of basketball. For me, I could've played anywhere there was a 10-foot hoop as long as I could play great basketball and make good money. I was playing great basketball but had no peace outside of it. Exodus 20:4-5 states, *"'You must not make any idols. Don't make any statues or pictures of anything up in the sky or of anything on the earth or of anything down in the water. Don't worship or serve idols of any kind, because I the Lord am your God.'"* Here, God is speaking of literal idols that you will also see in different countries as well as your own, but not adhering to these verses caused me a lot of pain and distress. I made basketball my idol to the point I would risk anything to be the best, to make money, and to play the way I knew I could play. But with that bad decision, the world was unveiled to me, removing my ignorance. The next season, at about age 27, I was in Argentina and there was a huge strike at the domestic airports. My teammate and I had just gotten cut and had to fly back to the States but instead of flying from our city to Buenos Aires to take the international flight, we had to drive 11 hours to the airport. It was crazy. When I got home to St. Louis, Missouri, the young man in Ferguson had just been killed so there were military vehicles and boarded-up shops everywhere. I was home for Thanksgiving week seeing all of the aftermath of the Black Lives Matter Movement but still had to be mentally ready to fly to Italy at the end of the week to finish the season. So much happens to us directly and indirectly due to the politics in a country. We cannot avoid much of it but it is important to have a basic understanding of what is going on to avoid taking deals in countries with issues we're not willing to deal with and also to prepare ourselves for how to deal with what is going on in a particular country. Remember, you are a child of God and this needs to be considered first when moving anywhere, especially out of the country.

Historical Territories

Now, we will transition into historical territories. As mentioned above, each country has its own rich history. From an American perspective, many of us have been taught a small portion of our country's history consisting of Columbus, manifest destiny, slavery, etc. Very little is taught about the ancient history of this region before our country was named the USA and, in some cases, the information we are taught is not true. Also, many of the negative things our nation has done abroad are not talked about in our schools or media so when walking into another country as a ball player, we have little to no knowledge of these things. I learned more about American history in other countries from people half my age than I ever did in any classroom in school growing up. If you want to know more about your bad qualities, ask your enemies. Overseas, there may be times when certain historical conversations come up based on a current issue or there may be times when someone challenges another based on their country's history or their personal history.

In Europe, many people will ask you first about your nationality, then about your origin. For people of African descent, whether it be African American, Afro Caribbean, Afro European, etc., you probably won't know your origin due to slavery. Some people may verbally attack you because of what your home country did to their country before they were born (or currently) which may be affecting them now. Most people will probably know nothing about this, and in some cases won't care to know. It's possible to feel empathetic or sympathetic to a person's struggle or frustration with your presence as being viewed as a foreign enemy to them. In any case, be careful to avoid such people and not be drawn into their conversations as you are still on foreign soil and you plan to finish the season in this country without issues. Let your team know right away if you're experiencing people trying to pull you into their drama. Understand and know that playing outside of the USA is not like playing in the NBA or the National Collegiate Athletic Association. There won't be an entourage of friends with you or a hired security guard to protect you from fanatical people. People will be able to get to you like a high school player. Many of the countries outside of the states are much older than the USA with thousands of years of history: older buildings, ancient native languages, different wars, conflicts, slavery, and colonization, to mention a few. Everyone will have a story that will rival your country's history and people will be prideful of their country just as you may be prideful of your country no matter how good or bad it is.

Wealthy nations and poverty-stricken nations have people who love their country, their national teams, and their heritages. Playing abroad exposes players to histories and details about histories that an athlete may have never known were true as many friends and teammates in those countries' families lived through wars, famine, and other historical events that you may have read about in history books. Their details will be deep and can make you feel positive or negative. Understand and know that God has made us all powerful to overcome all obstacles. You will understand more and more about the power of God when you learn other people's histories, as God created this world and the people and creatures in it. Do your best to see things out of God's lens and not your own. Don't become so smart that you become stupid and cannot see what is in front of you. As a world traveler, you may be privy to information others will not have access to, and conversations will change over time to the point where many people back home may become threatened or offended by what you know and speak of. There may be times when basic conversations will be outgrown with family and friends because of your exposure to the world, but do your best to be humble and balanced because there is still so much you don't know.

> *"Do not deceive yourselves. If any of you think you are wise by the standards of this age, you should become "fools" so that you may become wise. For the wisdom of this world is foolishness in God's sight. As it is written: "He catches the wise in their craftiness"; and again, "The Lord knows that the thoughts of the wise are futile"*
> *(1 Corinthians 3:18-20 NIV).*

This scripture sums up what can happen to anyone who travels and has major exposure. As an athlete, you are typically above normal consequences for bad decisions but not as many as you may think. Most of your interactions with people will be seasonal, so there are no years to gain a real understanding of who you're dealing with or what information you've come across.

When learning other people's histories, be sure not to open too many doors. If history becomes a person's idol, then they can open themselves up to too much information which may or may not be true, and too much information can make a person too emotional, unforgiving, cynical, and pessimistic. All these can be snares for the enemy to produce strongholds.

I can remember learning about my heritage at age 29. On one end it was very powerful and made me proud about coming from a strong people, and on the other end it angered me because of what happened to my family and who was involved in it. When learning history, no one's hands are clean. There is always someone to be upset with, including yourself, when looking at a person's history. Be careful not to buy into historical information that is contrary to the Word of God, because this can lead you down a dark path. Yes, Christianity is a young religion, but God is forever. There are historical documents that predate the Bible, but none predate God. Every place traveled will have stories of people and whichever god they serve, and those stories can be interesting and powerful. The stories will have a lot of information to back up their beliefs that will also sound convincing.

Let me share a piece of truth I learned the hard way; there is a difference between facts and the truth. Facts are what people commonly accept as reality, facts can change over time, depending on newfound knowledge. Truth remains the same no matter the age. God is truth, and facts are man's findings. A man can show up with tons of books and evidence to prove a finding or debunk someone. But when the wolf (devil) comes, God's truth will show up and man's facts will sit down. Remember you are a Christian, baptized in the blood of Jesus (who was not born of Adam, meaning he did not bear the curse of Adam's sin). Historically and currently, people have and will continue to pick apart the Bible. I have been there, but when the chips are down and we cry out to the Lord, He will answer us in the mightiest of ways. Once again, do not become so smart that you become stupid. The devil hides behind facts perceived as truth. As some people debunk the Bible and we listen to people skillfully debunk the Bible, the enemy swoops in like a hawk for the kill. Revelations 12:9 mentions how the devil was thrown down to the earth with his angels. Understand those fallen angels are here on earth and they know the word and what to say to entice a person to turn away or believe in other ways. Those angels having come from Heaven would also be powerful to us humans in a way to make them seem like deities and as we see in the Old Testament Book of Exodus, it is easy for mankind to turn away from God and worship others. This basic information is not to startle anyone or their family from pursuing your career overseas or out of state, it is just to make you aware of what is happening in different places and, quite frankly, this is probably happening at home as well. Have no fear of any opposition because God has given you authority over the enemy.

> *"I have given you authority to trample on snakes and scorpions and to overcome all the power of the enemy; nothing will harm you" (Luke 10:19 NIV).*

If you ever come across ungodly information that unsettles your spirit whether you hear it or see it, rebuke that information immediately in the name of Jesus. If you ever find yourself engulfed in any group that speaks against the Word of God, leave that group, renounce them in the name of Jesus, and inquire with a trusted pastor about deliverance as many doors may need to be closed. If anyone has fallen into this sort of trap, they need not feel ashamed or embarrassed to the point that they do not ask a trusted pastor or elder for help because it is their job to handle spiritual matters and the troubled person's story is probably not heavier than what a pastor or elder has experienced. Know that God will always forgive you, and when He forgives you, be sure to repent.

> *"If we confess our sins, he is faithful and just and will forgive us our sins and purify us from all unrighteousness" (1 John 1:9 NIV).*

Cultural Territories

Culturally, there are a myriad of ways people think and live. From upbringing to music, to food, and so on. Everyone has their particular way of doing things based on their heritage, history, traditions, or spirituality. One of the biggest challenges any foreigner will experience is culture. For example, many American basketball players have difficulty understanding why they're not allowed to dominate every game like we do in the USA. In the USA, the top three players on most teams take all of the shots and the entire system is built around those top players because it gives the team the best opportunity to win games. In America, we're capitalists which is about competition, outworking people to be the best, and being the best yields better finances and recognition in most cases.

In Europe, Australia, South America, and several other markets, what many players find is that those outside of the states are not capitalists economically or mentally. Many are socialists making people believe everyone is equal. In sports, this is not the best way to go about things in America because the reality is some players are better than others. Many times there are players (both local and foreign) who have the capability of averaging big numbers statistically but they're not given priority offensively or given a lot of playing time to reach those numbers consistently. In many places being a big scorer is viewed as selfish, which in many cases is not true, and consistently having huge games is frowned upon in certain markets. This is the culture of overseas sports except Asian markets and a handful of teams in various leagues throughout the world. When a player dominates the ball, even if it's necessary to win for a particular team, that player faces more scrutiny from teammates than we're accustomed to in the States. Does everyone on American teams like it when one or two players dominate the ball? No, but the players know that those players are typically the best and have to accept their role to continue on that team. Internationally, many times coaches are at the whim of domestic players who have heavy influence over the coach, and if the domestic players have an issue with a foreign player's style of play or ability, the foreign player will be forced to conform to a certain extent and can face loss of playing time, being frozen out of the play and in some cases be released from the team. Having limits on the number of foreign players (regardless of whether they're American or not) on each team leaves the foreign players at the whim of domestic players who may or may not like their presence on the team. To Americans, this can appear much like American sports in the early to mid-1900s when

African Americans were limited in their spots and roles on teams in sports. America has moved forward in this regard allowing players from anywhere in the world to have success no matter their nationality, race, religion, etc. In America, there are no rules that limit the amount of foreign players on a team and this tends to upset and confuse American-born players because of mistreatment on teams abroad. This also influences American players to adopt a mercenary mentality instead of being more prideful about their organizations due to the realities of being in the business of international sports. This is the business culture of sports overseas.

Outside of the business, there are different ways of doing things. I remember living in an Arabic country and hearing a horn sound five times per day for prayer. This horn could be heard all over the city, and immediately people would drop everything, lay out their rugs, and begin to pray. My teammates would pray together before every game, much like in the States before the new rules were put in prohibiting prayer. We (the American players) weren't forced to pray but outside of the American players, everyone was Muslim so they did what any other people dedicated to faith would do and follow their practices. In West Africa, there are many rules similar to home training in the USA. The elders make the decisions for the family; you must not speak to anyone in the morning before washing your face, you must speak to everyone the first time you see them in the morning, etc. In France, it is considered rude to speak about a person's financial ambitions or show too much anger. All of these small details go a long way and will begin to become a part of a person the longer they live somewhere. The music is different and the food can be different as well. Everyone is very passionate about their music and food so do not speak negatively about this.

But don't think people in foreign countries are some sort of alien species. I remember one summer I was home in Clarksville, Tennessee; I was in my mid-20s and saw a kid from my alma mater at a grocery store.

He asked me about overseas and I told him a few things and somehow we got on the subject of food. The teenage boy asked jokingly but with curiosity, "What do y'all eat over there? Y'all don't eat real food, do you?!" I chuckled and said, "Yeah man, we do... And we drink water, too." The food such as seasoning may be different, or the preparation, or different kinds of fruits and vegetables that may not grow in your home country, etc. But people worldwide eat chicken, turkey, duck, lamb, fish, and such. We all are still human beings. Some places may have more of a vegetarian or vegan population but people still eat many of the foods anyone is accustomed to eating.

One of the big things not to do in countries outside of the USA is to speak negatively about their heroes. In the States, we have hundreds of big-name celebrities, champions, and so on. Most countries outside of the USA are smaller, so there may only be a handful of world-renowned names from their nation so their countrymen support them 1000% and it's best not to speak negatively about any of them publicly or you may put yourself in immediate danger or risk being fired. I've seen this happen to players throughout the years. I remember playing in Argentina when they had a boxer facing off against an American boxer for the world championship in Las Vegas and people in Argentina would ask my American teammates and I whom we thought would win. The way they would ask is as if there would be trouble if we weren't for their guy. I've also experienced this in France when people asked about one of the French players being drafted as compared to one of the top American players. This can seem a bit strange for Americans because we don't have the same pride in our champions. After all, we have a lot more celebrities to choose from but in foreign nations, they may only have one or two world champions in the history of their entire country in any sport. I've also seen players make negative remarks about heroes from other countries while playing in those countries and get immediately banned from the league they were playing in. It's not a game.

Another big cultural difference is freedom of speech or the lack of it. Every country outside of the USA is not a freedom-of-speech country. In many places, a person can be locked up or killed for running their mouth about politics and powerful people. When out of the country, it's best to keep your mouth shut about these sorts of matters until you understand where you are and who you're talking to. I remember living in North Africa for one year and it was widely known in the country I was living in that you can speak against God but not the president or you would be exiled or imprisoned for five years. Speaking against politicians and powerful people has harsh penalties in many places outside of the United States. This is one reason why freedom of speech is fought for so hard in America, as a person's voice is a source of power. Understand that you are not special in the eyes of many foreigners simply because you are foreign or because you're an athlete. Many people will be in awe of foreign athletes and support them because they are foreign athletes playing for their team, but many people will hate them all the same. I remember an American player got killed in a club in Romania the year I played in Austria; the guy was only 23 years old. We were informed he was talking to a local woman in the club and the locals were jealous. It was conveyed to us he was told to leave her alone and the young man responded the way most American men would and he got killed. In Austria, where I was playing that season, a veteran American player was in a similar situation at a club talking to an Austrian woman. We were informed similarly, the locals didn't like it and the American player responded aggressively. The local just so happened to be a kickboxer and he kicked the man's knee backward and ended his season. These sorts of things happen in and out of the country, and you need to be aware of your surroundings whether you're an athlete or not. I've seen local players get beaten up by other locals over women in clubs as well. As a popular athlete (public figure), you will face heightened jealousy that people with normal jobs typically don't face because they're not as visible in the community. Many people don't have dating options, or access to certain groups or clubs, etc., and hate to see someone like you show up in their city/state/country and instantly have it all, so you need to be aware of your surroundings. Have fun, meet people, and try new things, but have some awareness of those around you.

Be sure to check in with your home nation's embassy. In a foreign country, there might be issues that would require you to do so. Checking in with an embassy online will give anyone basic information about the country they're going to with live updates, warnings, resources, and so forth. If the country you are going to doesn't have an embassy from your home country, this can be a bad sign as your native country may not have a great relationship with the country of residence. This doesn't mean that every country with an embassy from your home country is safe, but it does mean that if troubles arise, and you're registered with that embassy, the embassy will send immediate updates on what to do and when to do it right away.

The Pastors' Take on Friendships in Different Cultures

Bishop Lelton Davis
Mesa, Arizona, USA

Question

How does a young person with little experience deal with people from other cultures who practice various spiritualities?

Bishop Davis' response:

A lot of times the enemy works through being lame, dormant, and hiding, he does not expose himself. So, a lot of times people think that, "Oh! It's just innocent, it's just entertainment, or it's just a game." The devil is very good in music and movies, he loves to hide in things that he knows will enter into your eye gate and ear gate. So, someone young might be watching demonic movies and think, "Oh, it's just a movie, it's just entertainment." Or they're listening to music that degrades women and talks about killing and all kinds of stuff that gives those demons the right to be raging in your life.

As a young person, whether you're dating or trying to be alive for Christ, you will find it uncomfortable to claim Christ. Now you feel ashamed, you don't want to be looked at as a 'church boy' or corny, so it's easy to hide because everything that God does is in the light. We (Christians) don't have to hide; we expose everything done in the dark. So sometimes to be cool they may try something and unfortunately get addicted to it, because they don't want to seem lame at a party. "Oh, you don't drink, you don't smoke, you're not cool, you're not this, you're not that."

As a young person, the first thing you should do is establish yourself as a leader. You should also get delivered from the opinion of people. Because if not, you can be swayed to and fro.

If I'm (you're) young and I'm (you're) trying to seek God, I (you) cannot be afraid to go against the grain. Broad is the way that leadeth to destruction. It's important that as a young person you begin leadership training. At every level, there should be some kind of leadership, if not you'll become a follower.

> *"You can enter God's Kingdom only through the narrow gate. The highway to hell is broad, and its gate is wide for the many who choose that way. But the gateway to life is very narrow and the road is difficult, and only a few ever find it"* *(Matthew 7:13-14 NLT).*

Advice on Entering a New Culture

Pastor Juma Nashon
Nairobi, Kenya

Pastor Juma Explains

If you're going somewhere you have never been, you are going to have culture shock. You are going to experience meeting people differently than what you are used to. It's always important that you have a rough idea of where you are going. Research is key and being in Christ means that you are going to make certain choices. Not everywhere is an environment that can build you so you are going to make certain choices and this may come by having certain knowledge about a place. You can research and get it or you can also get a referral. In your country, somebody may have visited that place. Being a Christian, you are also going to rely on your relationship, fellowship, and prayer. When you identify with Christ, some of the basic key things you are taught are how to pray and to read the Word of God. This should enable you and empower you to have spiritual guidance. Where you go, there are also authorities, and most times foreigners are always targets. They (you) may be a target for manipulation, and they (you) may be a target for harm. It's always good that you stay in contact with authorities, they can give you information on where to walk and where not to walk, where to go and where not to go, and where to associate and where not to associate.

Pastor Christopher Deletsa
Lille, France

Pastor Christopher Explains Different Cultures

Know yourself, know your personality. Who are you when you have nothing else? When I moved from Ghana to France, it was a different system. Everything was different. I had culture shock, having conversations with people was different. The words you say to people, you can't say the same way, the delivery is different. You have to find yourself in Christ first, then when you move to that new environment, now you know yourself and build in that environment. That environment should not influence you; you should influence that environment. Study the environment, study the culture. The Word of God doesn't change, but it can help you to fit into a system. I cannot use the same way of evangelism back home in Ghana, in France. Even in France the various departments have different ways of living. So first you need to know who you are, have in your hand I know who I am in Christ, I know my duty as a Christian. Now that you come here (France) or to another country and do not know your purpose, you'll be influenced.

Purpose can be realized in the place God is sending you to. For example, in the story of Jonah, God sent (Jonah) to this country. It is that place where you have to realize your purpose. But what happens if you don't know your purpose when you move into that country? Now the culture of that country influences your purpose, which is not bad. You can find your purpose where you arrive. But it will be best if you find your purpose before moving to that place. In that way, your purpose will not be influenced. When the Bible says to study yourself approved, it is not just studying the Word of God. Study people, study culture, study society. In every knowledge, except the knowledge of God, there are loopholes. How do I (you) use this knowledge to realize my (your) purpose here?

Racial Territories

Disclaimer

This section contains profanity I commonly used in this stage of my life. I chose to write the words exactly how they were spoken and thought of during this period of time for the benefit of readers who need the truth to be conveyed for their betterment.

This section about race may be the most controversial of any section in this book as racial issues open many wounds and stir up many emotions.

One of the common questions I get from Americans when I come home is, "Is it racist overseas?" There is a movement of people leaving the States to go to other nations based on their opinions and experiences of racism in America. I cannot speak for everyone's situations but from my experiences abroad, I've never faced extreme racism until I left the USA. In the States, we focus on racism as our country was built on it and it's pumped into our psyche through media, but the reality is most countries on this planet were built on some form of slavery of domestic and/or foreign people. What makes America's racism unique is not the slave trade in the USA, because during that time the world mandate was to exclusively enslave Africans as opposed to other people. Before this mandate was made, anyone of any race could be enslaved. This had much to do with the conflicts of Africans with other Africans on the continent of Africa through political and tribal conflicts along with foreigners from other continents looking to build their nations and increase trade-off free labor. In efforts to depopulate Africa, and weaken their empires, along with the fact that Africans could handle the harsh conditions of the voyages, living quarters, and workloads, Africans were under siege both on the continent of Africa and abroad. It was upsetting for me to learn from tribal leaders that Africans had their ships and crossed the Atlantic Ocean to sell Africans hundreds of years before Europeans did. There are other racial impacts such as colonization, wars, and so on that also affect the world we live in today. You can find racism throughout the Bible and many other religious books and cultures throughout the earth. Racism is something we all have to deal with in one way or another.

What makes racism in the USA unique is the freeing of the slaves prompting other nationalities identified as white to form a more powerful group to combat the freed Africans who no longer could identify with a nation or tribe as their history was beaten out of them. Much like how we vote and change policies that are linked to blocks such as the black vote, the Hispanic vote, the Asian vote, and so on, the USA has different nationalities present among people who consider themselves white. During slave times, Caucasians identified with their countries of origin such as French, Portuguese, Lithuanian, etc. They were not necessarily friends or enemies at the time, but each group migrated to America and had their own needs and ambitions just like any other nationality. The biggest threat to those groups was having millions of freed Africans in America with labor skills such as carpentry, agriculture, and mechanics. Those 1st, 2nd, and 3rd generation African Americans no longer knew their home countries or tribal history, so they had to identify with each other because they were in the same struggle. This created a large voting block along with a large group of people who would be able to work together to get their needs met and was feared by their former enslavers. This is when labor unions and more systems were created to lock out people of African descent along with other people such as native Americans, people of Latin American heritage, and so on. So, during that time, the identity of a person was no longer whether they were English, Belgian, or Italian, they identified as 'white' to have a bigger block of influence for politics and trade and many of those systems are still in effect today.

Moving on, I also want to explain that everything is not racist. For example, if someone calls another person a derogatory term or stereotypes of their racial background, this is not racism but prejudice. Many times, we put racism on top of prejudice. Prejudice, although upsetting, does not majorly affect people the same way as racism does. Prejudice is more of a person letting others know that they don't like them because they are different. Racism is a system and/or group that will not allow a person to make a living or live somewhere because they are different. Prejudice impacts a person's emotions; whereas racism impacts a person's emotions, family, well-being, generational wealth, and so on. Most people can deal with prejudice, but dealing with racism is much more difficult to overcome. A person needs to know the difference so they can fight more meaningful battles of substance than worrying about what others think of them. There will be people who treat us differently both good and bad because we're athletes, because we're a certain race, religion, language, profession, and so on. Unfortunately, this is human nature to judge people based on their appearance, profession, finances, etc. This can be frustrating because a racist system minimizes opportunities for certain people much like having a limit on how many foreigners can be on a team internationally.

Racism, as it stands, is a challenging plight to overcome but here is some insight as to how it works so you can prepare yourself for the world. What I can tell you is that racism has many forms in many nations across this planet and from my experience racism has one major difference from the USA to most other nations. The difference is that the state's racism is color-based whereas in other nations racism's first level is nationality-based, then color-based comes second. When it comes to territories, your racial background matters in most places.

Speaking from the USA perspective, as an American going overseas to play, you must understand that there is a built-in racial boundary (regardless of your color) which you may not notice as racism upfront. It took most of us (Americans) years to realize the racial boundary to only allow a specific number of Americans on a roster as compared to domestic players when this is simply not a way of life in America. In America, we don't have rules on the books preventing foreign players from playing any sport. In America, we don't care where a person is from. If they can do the job, we put the ball in their hands and let them go. This is evident in all of our sports on every level. This does not mean racism doesn't exist in the USA or in our sports because it does, but it has progressed beyond archaic boundaries that the rest of the world has not surpassed at this point. As the rise of foreign players continues to grow in the states, I've experienced some countries decrease their limits of American players slowly from 4 to 3 to 2 to 1 Americans permitted on a team in some places. There are also other roster spots made for foreigners from other European countries called Bosman or Cotonou who are foreigners born in colonized African/Caribbean countries. Bosman and Cotonou are also limited on an international roster with usually one or two spots. From my experience, it's a lot like what I've been educated about when the American professional leagues first started to allow African American players into the pros. In many places, Americans are the first ones cut from the team if the team loses, and there are a lot of players whose payments come late or not at all depending on the country and team. Americans can be mistreated off the court by prejudiced people who may judge us due to what's portrayed on television and so on. There are countless stories and situations that any athlete from America or otherwise can share about being mistreated in foreign countries and it will have very little to do with your color but mostly to do with your nationality. People foreign to America and other countries will also have their own stories about being mistreated racially as they're affected as well. Internationally, it will come down to your nationality first then your origin. People will typically ask what your nationality is (your home country) and then what your origin is (your heritage country). This is the basic data for a person to know what box to put a person in. Many African Americans/Afro-Latinos and others affected by the Atlantic slave trade do not know their origin country. I will discuss the importance of knowing your origin country later. After all, knowing your origin is key in international sports markets. A person will be treated at large by their nationality first then their color second. Most people will be in awe of you as a foreigner in general, especially as an American, because of everything people see in movies, sports, and entertainment. We are a unique people with certain freedoms and privileges that many countries do not have like freedom of speech, freedom of religion, the right to bear arms, and so on. Many places do not have these basic rights and this can also make you a target from the time you land in a foreign country based on how a person feels about these topics.

I remember my first flight as a pro headed overseas. I was 22 and my dad told my mom he would take me to the airport instead of her. This was a proud moment for my dad to see his baby boy get his first job. We got everything all checked in and he walked with me to the security gate and said, "Well, son, I've taught you all I know, you're your own man now. STAY OFF THE TITTY!" I headed on to the plane like I had done many times before but this flight was a bit different as I was confronted and insulted by a middle-aged Finnish man. There was a vacant aisle seat in front of me that I was planning to take as it had more leg room but unfortunately, this man took the seat in front of me before I could get to it. Not much longer into the flight as I was minding my business watching a movie in the entertainment center in front of me, the man tried to put his seat back abruptly which instantly hit my knees strongly. I tapped him on the shoulder and politely asked him to move his seat up because it was hurting my knees. At first, he acted as if I didn't say anything to him, so I tapped him again and repeated myself. The man reluctantly moved his seat up. About 30 minutes later, I was watching a movie with my headset on and I sensed someone standing at my left side. I didn't think much of it because why would anyone be worried about me on the plane? In any case, after about 20 seconds, I noticed this person was still hovering over me to the left (I was in the middle row on the aisle seat just behind the emergency row aisle seat). I eventually looked up to see why someone was still standing next to me and noticed this person had an angry look on his face and was looking directly at me. In confusion, I took my headset off and said, "What's up?" The man then told me in his accent, "Before, you asked me to move my seat up and I complied, but now I'm going to move my seat back and you're not going to do anything about it." Anyone who knew me at the age of 22 knew that would have an immediate pushback from me. I couldn't believe this man dared to say this to me as if it was acceptable, it was so offensive the girl sitting to my right was thrown off by it too. I immediately unbuckled my seat belt, got up eye to eye with this man, and told him, "You ain't going to do s***." Then we had some words and he rushed to his seat to put his seat back. I sat on my seat and forced his seat to stay up, then he got up again which I also did because I didn't know if this man was going to attack me or not. However, he rushed back to his seat again and I returned to mine, but still held his seat up. Eventually, he rose from his seat again and I did, too. We were eye to eye but the girl sitting next to me suddenly intervened, "You can sit in my seat and he can have his seat back." I told her, "No, you're not moving anywhere. He's going to keep his seat up." So this man who was also my height of 6'4" and wider than me at the time (he was about 245lbs and I was 225lbs), started to ask me questions that were very insulting to me. "What's your name?" He asked me. "Don't worry about what my name is," I replied. "I know why you're coming here (to Finland)." As if to say the only reason a black man is going to Finland is to play sports. "What's it to you? Why are you worried about where I'm going?" was my response. The man asked, "What school did you attend?" He asked me this several times. I responded with, "What difference does it make?" He then said, "Well, I went to Minnesota and that's a big school," and before he could say anything to try to downplay my abilities as an athlete based on being a high/mid/low major, I answered, "Well I know a lot of f***ing idiots that went to Minnesota and I'm talking to one right now." He was shocked by my intelligence and the fact that I refrained from striking him, which seemed to be his expectation. It appeared he wanted to prove that I fit the stereotype of a black man unable to control himself, as often depicted on television shows. For about an hour, we exchanged insults while 30,000 feet in the air, and remarkably, no one else seemed to notice the tension except for the girl seated next to me. I made a conscious effort to keep my voice steady and calm. Despite the intensity of the situation, this man showed no signs of weakness. I, too, remained composed. After a while, he finally said, "Okay, you win, you're young." Then, what he said after that was with the tone of a real gangster, "I hope you spend a long time in Finland… Watch your back in Finland." Afterward, he sat down next to his family and left me alone. When he said those last words, it sent chills through me because I started to realize he may have been on the streets out there, his build, his mentality, his tactics, etc. All I could think was, man, I'm about to go out here not knowing anyone and I already have enemies. After the plane landed, we crossed paths several times and headed to baggage claim and customs; it was an eerie feeling. When I got off the plane in Finland walking to my layover flight, 90% of the people in the airport stared at me everywhere I walked. This was not the look of people in awe of an athlete but people staring because they'd never seen a black man before. I felt uncomfortable and different. When I arrived, the team didn't uphold the contract. I had no apartment and stayed in another player's room on a twin bed, had no winter coat in Finland (one of the coldest countries on the planet). I got cut because the league only allowed three Americans on a team, which is racist in and of itself.

As an overseas player, there may be times when you as a foreigner arrive on a team and you're treated like a second-class citizen, even though you're the best player on the team. Teams may tell you that you're the man for the job and then you arrive and two or three other players are competing with you for the spot that you knew nothing about. Honesty is hard to come by in competitive sports, no matter the league.

Moving on, I played in France for the longest amount of time, roughly seven years on and off. I had some of the best times of my life there and some of the worst times of my life there. France was the country that made me pay attention to racism the most because I started to learn more about myself as an African American. This was because every team I played for had people of African descent on them from Africa, Europe, South America, and the Caribbean. Many of them knew their home countries and tribes and they behaved much differently than folks back home. I was intrigued by them and asked many questions about their cultures. I began to understand the importance of knowing where you're from, not just from a business aspect but from a self-identity aspect. Interestingly enough, the same barriers that keep black men divided in life are barriers in sports as well as politically, psychologically, and so on. Here we are all of African descent and we all have something negative to say about one another in certain situations. I noticed that many times when things go wrong with the team, the Africans born in Africa go to their corner, the Africans born in Europe go to their corner, Afro-Caribbeans go to their side, and African Americans go to their side. I could see in real-time just how much damage we've done to one another and how much damage others have done to us which keeps us divided. Along with the rules that are in place such as three Americans (typically African Americans) on a team, two Cotonou on a team, and unlimited domestic players on a team. When a team begins to lose, and it doesn't matter the country, the foreign players will take the blame first, typically the Americans. Many domestic players won't admit this, but they know it. The chances of an American player getting cut overseas are high if your team is losing or if the domestic players don't like you. It's a lot like the American sports leagues when African American players were being integrated into different sports leagues. France is good to live race-wise because there is more diversity, similar to the USA. Racism is more systematic in sports and it's not necessarily color-based, it's nationality-based. A person may not treat another person differently because they are black or white or Arab or Asian; they may treat them differently due to their home country or country of origin. I've met many Europeans who are Caucasians and will correct you immediately if they're called white because they don't want to be misconstrued with Caucasian Americans, they identify with their country. This is the same with people from Africa, they will tell you not to call them Africans, as they identify with their home country. It doesn't matter whether you're an African American, Asian American, Hispanic American, etc., you still count as American on the roster and you'll still be the first one shipped out if things go wrong during the season; it's just how it is. This is one of the toughest things for American players to grasp overseas because in America we don't care where you're from if you can play, we're all looking to win no matter where you're from, but outside of the USA this is not a reality in most places. Germany is the only country outside of the USA that does not have a limit on how many Americans are on a team. Outside of the challenges of the sport, I didn't have many issues with race off the court in France. I can only remember one time when I was treated shabbily because of my color. I was at a train station about to buy a ticket to Paris and the ticket machines were broken, so I had to get on the train without a ticket. I figured I would just tell the ticket checker the situation and pay for my ticket on the train. When the ticket man came around, I explained the situation and pulled out my credit card to pay. Unfortunately, the ticket checker did not give me any mind and told me that no one told them the ticket machines were broken and I had to pay a fine. I pleaded my case telling him, "Hey, man, I didn't hide anything from you, I pulled out my credit card ready to pay." He didn't care about anything I was saying and gave me the energy of someone who thought I was just another n*gg** hopping on trains. I refused to pay the fine and he went and got the security. I ended up having to pay the fine and I was so angry I followed him for 10 minutes when we got off the train because I was going to take my money back when the security left him but fortunately for us both the police never left his side. I've had other racist things happen to me on several teams but I won't go too deep into those stories to protect the people I care about on those teams and to keep some things private. This book is not meant to smear team or player names but is to give readers insight into how to navigate foreign territories.

Going further east for an African American can be more challenging depending on how docile, knowledgeable, or caring of a person you are or not. Austria was similar to Finland in some ways as many times I received stares from people who were curious to see someone like me who is different. I cannot be upset about this because I too have seen different kinds of people in my travels that I've never seen before and looked at them curiously. I think this is unfortunately natural for many of us, and not all of these stares are meant to be derogatory. Many people are in awe of your look, your skin, your hair, your demeanor, etc. Foreigners are exotic to domestic people, no different than a foreigner coming to America and we look at them with intrigue at times. Although this is a natural occurrence for many, this is not polite in every situation and can still impact people who experience these stares as if they're part of a carnival show. I experienced this a bit in Austria.

I can remember seeing an African man in the grocery store next to my apartment and he gave me a look of shock as if he thought he was the only black man around there. I had many rough experiences in Austria and my experiences in Austria led to the dismantling of my faith during that time. I dominated the first two months of the season and after a while I started being called for travels, getting in foul trouble, and all sorts of obviously flagrant bad calls to slow me down from dominating. For a time, as a competitor, we tend to watch films, make adjustments to do better, and avoid these calls. But after this continued for several games and I had made a noticeable adjustment, I knew that I was being treated unfairly. There are times when refs will laugh at your frustration overseas or allow you to be fouled hard with no calls because you're American. You will be hard-pressed to find an American player who's played multiple years abroad and will not have stories like this. The other issue Americans tend to face overseas is being benched or frozen out of games by coaches and players. The reality is the jealousy of a foreign player coming over and dominating game after game bothers a lot of domestic players to the point where there are complaints to the coaching staff and the coach is influenced to limit the player's minutes or touches. This happens even when the coaches know it is not the best thing for them to do. They don't want to lose their jobs. Except in Asia and Middle Eastern markets, along with a few teams in each league, it's common to see countless players averaging 20+ points, 10+ rebounds, and 10+ assists the first five to ten games of the season and by January/February those numbers drop significantly due to minutes going down and touches going down. Many teams begin to lose because of these decisions and foreign players lose their jobs first unless the coach and general manager are powerful and serious about winning. I've also played for coaches that didn't allow this sort of thing and we were able to win more. I played for over a decade internationally and there was only one coach that defended me against domestic players in the heat of the situation and only one team that racism wasn't an issue. The benching and lowering of touches to American players is a difficult pill to swallow because we are capitalists and we're about winning. Americans do not care who the best player is or where they're from, we are trained to win and put the ball in the hands of the best players so we can win championships and anything outside of that is frowned upon. In many cases, foreign nations are more concerned with building their countrymen than winning a championship, which isn't necessarily a bad thing from their perspective, but this doesn't bow so well for foreign players. Unfortunately, many times these barriers create an undercurrent of built-in dissension and animosity that can be difficult to overcome.

Moving back to Austria, I remember a game when I grabbed a rebound, chinned the ball as we're taught in America, and my elbow caught one of the Austrian players as he was swiping at the ball. He didn't get hit hard, but forceful enough for him to know he wasn't getting the ball. I noticed his body language was more aggressive towards me so I kept my eye on him as we ran down the floor. As we neared half court this guy swung on me, his fist grazed my face, I pushed him away from me and squared up with him. The game then stopped and I was ejected from the game and my coach and everyone yelled at me like I was in the wrong. The second guy always gets caught. The next day, the front office told me that if I ever acted like that again, I'd be fined and suspended and the fine would be so big that I wouldn't recover. It seemed as if they didn't view me as a person, like I was just a foreign n*gg*r who was supposed to shut up, make them money, and allow myself to be attacked. I told him: "I flew over here thousands of miles away from my family and friends and someone attacked me on our home floor and you took his side against me?! Don't you ever talk to me like this again, I don't need you. If a man attacks me on the floor, on the streets, even if it's you, I am going to defend myself." Then I walked out of the office. Later in the season, we were on a road trip coming home, and our team bus stopped at a gas station. We all went to grab some snacks and use the bathroom. I was learning Deutsch at the time and I ordered a sandwich in Deutsch to the best of my ability. The man taking the order told me, "You're American, speak English." So, then I ordered my food in English and then this man started yelling at me for not speaking his language. He was shouting at the top of his lungs in front of everyone, and I told my teammates, "See, man, this is what I have been talking about, people are racist out here." I was just 24 at the time and this was the first time I was so angry and disappointed like this. No local there understood how I felt because it wasn't their experience. I remember I got so angry with someone there that I contemplated killing him. I was tired of the mistreatment. My Mom called me while I was there on my magic jack and she asked how I was doing. I said, "Mom, if I see this guy today, I'm going to kill him." She said, "What?!" I said, "If I see this dude today, I'm going to strangle him to death, and murder him in cold blood." She stated frantically, "You're going to go to jail if you do that!!!" I replied, "Well, you better pray or something because if I see this dude, it's going down." She hung up on me. This is the damage of racism and prejudice to a man.

The worst thing that happened to me there was seeing a video of a slave dungeon in Africa that was controlled by so-called Christians who would capture slaves and force them to convert to Christianity before putting the chains back on them and shipping them to the Americas. To see the process of the men being brought out of the slave dungeon in chains, then being forced to kneel in front of a cross and being forced to say that Jesus died and rose again, only to have holy oil splashed on them did something to my spirit; it rocked me to the core. At 24 going through what I was going through already and then seeing this made me question everything about God, Christianity, and if it was for me. There was a shockwave that went through my entire body, I could not unsee this, for the next few years my trust in God and belief in Christianity had a gradual decline. No one at home could get through to me about this matter because no one I knew had these experiences or was willing to talk to me about their experiences like this. All I could do was try my best to bury it and play ball.

Playing in Arabic countries was mind-blowing as well. On one hand, basketball was going great and on the other, I was exposed to truths that I hope no one reading this book will ever have to be exposed to. I remember I signed late at age 26 and signed with a team in North Africa. I was excited to go to Africa and wondered what life would be like there. I had a long layover in Paris, so I left the airport and hung out a bit then flew to Tunisia City, a nice place, but training camp was further south in Sousa and that was very troubling. Sticking with this chapter's theme of racism, my understanding of it went to another level. Now my teammates were a mixture of Arabic men and African descent men and of course African Americans. We all decided to go to the beach on our day off and chill out on the shore of the Mediterranean Sea. All I could think was wow, my feet are on African soil and I'm on the other side of the Mediterranean facing Europe. I thought about my time in Antibes, France, looking towards Africa. All was good until we headed back to the hotel. My American teammate and I were a bit ahead of our Libyan teammates and I noticed a police van pull up slowly and one of the policemen was looking hard at us. Being from St. Louis and knowing how things can be, I kept my eyes forward and kept walking towards the hotel. My Libyan teammates didn't have the same success. The policeman stopped them and accused them of looking at the women on the beach. My American teammate and I were looking back at them, but a Tunisian man on the street told us very sternly to go to the hotel because the policeman was there to harass us. We couldn't understand his language but understood his body language as the man kept waving for us to go to the hotel. So, we went inside the hotel and looked out of the restaurant window to see what the problem was. The police detained my teammates, it didn't matter that one was black and the other Arabic, but it mattered they were Libyan. I couldn't believe this was happening.

Eventually, they were released and didn't go to jail or anything but it was just some silly intimidation about nothing. Coming from the States, I couldn't understand why anyone would care if someone was looking at a woman at all, let alone at a beach. Later, with the same team, I remember going to the airport in Egypt when we had a long layover. My coach was from Egypt so he took my American teammate and me to see the city, but our Libyan teammates couldn't leave the airport because of some conflict with Egypt. All I could think of was wow, how can you not be able to travel next door? It would be like Americans not being able to go to Canada or Mexico. Other than being in West Africa, I've never seen a person go through so much and have so much love towards one another. Those were some of the best teammates I ever had. I also remember when arriving in Libya at the customs station, the agent wouldn't let me enter the country for about 30 minutes. Our team president, GM, and coach all pleaded with the man and he said, "No, he's American!" It was a big deal and when I finally got through, my teammates surrounded me and escorted me through the airport outside. It was wild.

Italy offered similar racism that I experienced in other places. At age 27, I started with the team playing well and then a five-game span of getting in foul trouble unjustly happened. It always would happen in the 3rd or 4th quarter to prevent me from finishing the games. In the very last game I was in, I grabbed a rebound and one of the Italian players jumped on my back and had his arm around my neck trying to get the ball, then another Italian player grabbed my arm and stripped me of the ball. All I could think was how can someone jump on my back like a monkey and I not get the call? In the same play, they turned the ball over and my teammate passed me the ball for a layup. I saw the opposing Italian player's eyes looking to try to knock me out of the air, so I slowed down to absorb the blow before shooting. When the ref called the foul, I walked up to the Italian player and leaned towards his ear so he could hear me. I told him, "Don't think I won't f**k you up out here." The referee then ejected me from the game and told everyone that I head-butted the Italian player. A week after the game, I got a message that I had to pay a fine and serve a suspension for head-butting a player when the film clearly showed this didn't happen at all. I was just lighting them up offensively and they wanted that team to make the playoffs.

There was another situation off the court in Italy where I realized a fraction of people simply don't know or care about what they do as regards to racial imaging. One evening, a couple of my teammates and I went to a local restaurant to get some burgers. My teammates raved about this place all week saying the food was like America. So, I rode up there with my guys and as we pulled up, I noticed a confederate flag covering the entire window of the restaurant. In my eyes, having been raised in St. Louis, Missouri, I was in a very precarious situation. Do I go in and eat as if there's no problem? Is this flag a sign that this is a place I'm forbidden to enter? Do I tell my teammates to take me home and make everyone uncomfortable? I walked in with them and mentioned the flag to my teammates as I no longer wanted to eat at this place. They could see the displeasure in my face and the tone in which I spoke. Had I driven my car, I would've never entered the place and gone home. All I could think was how I'm over here and have to deal with this sh**. So, we're in line and I ask the guy at the register why they had a confederate flag in the window. He couldn't speak English, so I had my teammate translate everything. The young man at the register told me he thought it was cool because he saw it in a funny American movie. I told him that this flag is an insult to every black person in the States and I don't care about that movie. I made an order to not ruin the night for my teammates, but I couldn't bring myself to eat anything. When they dropped me off at my apartment I got into my car and drove back to the restaurant to give them back my food because my spirit was convicted. When I pulled up to the restaurant, they were closed and the flag was removed from the window. I didn't realize it until I was already out of the car with the food in my hand. The owner of the restaurant was an older Turkish man who spoke English and he walked directly up to me and asked if there was something wrong with my food. I told him I was just bringing it back because when they had the confederate flag up, I couldn't eat the food due to it being insulting to my people. The owner told me, "I asked the young man (his employee) what that situation was about and I told him to take it down because we don't do anything to insult our customers." He apologized for this mistake and insisted I take my food because he meant no harm and would never have allowed this if he knew what it represented. I went and sat in my car and thought for a few minutes about this situation and realized that there are a lot of people who are not about race or prejudice, we are just in a world where this sort of thing exists and we have to stand firm in our convictions. Maybe God wanted me to have this experience so that I could share it with readers. I don't know, but I was able to go home in peace without feeling negative about that place.

Argentina provided different challenges but more of the same. I was 27 at the time. The experience was very interesting. For example, they had Columbus Day but also on the same day, there was Indigenous Day. Many people didn't celebrate Columbus Day because when he arrived in South America, this signaled the demise of many of the natives who resided in Argentina. Although Columbus landed in Brazil just north of Argentina, his influence stretched beyond Brazil. Columbus' presence in South America also affected the Africans who arrived in South America before Columbus arrived as well. It is well-known in those areas that Columbus enslaved many of the natives in the areas he infiltrated. In the states, we typically focus solely on the slave trade in the northern hemisphere from America to Europe to Africa but the reality is two transatlantic slave trades were happening simultaneously, one in the northern hemisphere and the other in the southern hemisphere. Ships were packed with slaves in West Africa and shipped to the Caribbean as well as to Brazil in South America. Once these ships arrived in the Caribbean, depending on companies making the trades, slaves would be shipped across the southern border of the USA as well as up the east coast of the USA as well as throughout Central America. Throughout South America, slave ships went down the eastern coastline of the continent from as high as Guyana, Suriname, and French Guiana down to the lowest tip of Argentina and the Falkland Islands. When ships left the USA, they traveled back to Europe with slaves and other goods, back down to West Africa. In the southern hemisphere, ships left Argentina and the Falkland Islands to South Africa. One thing you will notice in South America is there are all sorts of people of African descent. This is due to the West Africans' arrival to Brazil long before

Columbus as well as the slave trade which came later. Travelers will see many people of African descent in Europe, Australia, and other places due to early African migrations and slave trades as well. Travelers may also meet families who live on different continents because their families were brought to those continents as slaves by Africans they were captured by. This is striking because in America we're only taught about European slave ships, but as I lived around the world, I became privy to certain truths that were hard to bear.

Moving on, in Argentina the racism I faced was overt by some and covert by others. Over that, some people would talk to me like I was uneducated or stupid. For example, when ordering a pizza, the delivery man would try to take advantage of my not knowing the currency exchange rate or the language. Sometimes people in the organization may say things to you that expose their lack of humanity towards you. In one game we were up double digits in the 3rd quarter and then all of the American players were benched for the entire 4th quarter. We lost by double digits and the team's president came downstairs into the locker room and met with all of the Americans to ask us why we lost as if it was our fault but none of us played in the 4th and when we were playing, we were killing the other team. The president spoke to us as if it was obvious we were the problem. The team never lived up to their contractual obligations, paying players foreign and domestic months late, not putting us in apartments like stated in our contracts, etc. We all stayed in hotels for the season which wasn't so bad, we got free meals all day and had suites, but there were a lot of quirky things that we couldn't expect coming from America. One thing is when we left for a road trip, we came back to the hotel and many times our luggage would be sitting in the lobby because the hotel management wanted to fill our rooms with other occupants. We would return to find our bags in the lobby and not our rooms. Other times if the hotel had more guests, they would take one of us out of our rooms and put us in the same room. We would come back from practice or games to find our clothes in each other's rooms. We (the American players) would tell our agents and the Argentinian agents would fight back against us saying they do a lot for race relations, etc. To complicate matters when our Argentinian teammates came to their hotel rooms, their bags were never removed and put out in the open like ours. We also had several times where we would have to pack up our bags and take them to a storage near the hotel until we returned. It was very prejudiced and disrespectful. We ended up boycotting the team due to lack of payment and they told us this is unprofessional. We even got cut from the team on the internet just after playing a game the night before when the coach and president acted like everything was all good, shook my hand looking me in the eyes. When we got cut, they forced us to leave abruptly with no time to get our clothes out of the laundromat. They told us we could stay until our clothes came, but we would have to pay for the hotel, food, travel to the airport, etc. The prices were crazy. To make matters worse, the domestic airports were on strike so they had a driver drive us 11 hours to the airport in Buenos Aires and we weren't shown which terminal to go to or anything. It was one of the most disrespectful things I endured in my career.

I've also had the blessing of traveling to West Africa on many occasions, and I've had some of the best times there and met some of the best people there. But their leagues have similar rules when it comes to Americans and other foreigners. There's a limit as to how many are on each team and although I know my family history down to the village, many Africans have called me white because I am light-skinned. I remember getting my passport and filling out all of the documents proving my family's migration to the States through our enslavement and forced voyage to the Caribbean and then to the States. Throughout family research, you will find many stories of our distant relatives who were raped by slave owners of different races which contributes to many African Americans' lighter skin tones. After finding this information at age 29, I found myself at the passport office a year later in the country of my heritage and the lady at the office indirectly insulted me in French. Talking to my translator she said, "What are you all trying to pull off here?! He isn't Malian, he's white!" She didn't know I spoke French and could understand everything she said, and I was angered by this.

Over the years, I've met and have many friends from the continent who think the same about many African Americans and other people of African descent who are lighter-skinned. Many call African Americans white as a joke like it's funny that our family members were sold off by people who raped them only to be purchased by other people of different races who raped them as well. It hit me differently because I researched for years to find my heritage, and the village, learned the language, met with historians and chiefs on the continent, met with my elders and I know the stories and hardships my family has overcome. Here I was, becoming the first American athlete in the history of Mali to play on the national team, and I received one of the biggest insults an African American could ever receive. But that's how the enemy works. The devil will work through other people to try to get you out of character. All I could think was how dare you insult me when Africans in Africa are the reason slavery existed in this land and it's your very own kinfolk that you're insulting. I know who raped their way into my family lineage. I've also been mistreated and faced prejudice and racism in other places throughout the years in Europe and Africa by Africans due to my being lighter skinned. I've also informed my fellow African Americans to stop insulting African people from the continent by making other derogatory remarks that they don't appreciate. It's as if spiritually both sides know there's an issue but they can't get to the root of it. It's an unfortunate reality that I hope changes someday.

The conclusion to racism and prejudice while living abroad is that you cannot escape it. It doesn't matter what country a person is from, what nationality they are, or their skin color. You will deal with racism and prejudice. There are countries I've lived in where white people are treated just as badly as black people in other countries. The reality is there are a lot of people on this planet who just don't like you, won't treat you right, and will do things to keep you down. Many of these sorts of people won't look like you and many of them will look like you. It is up to a person to use their discernment and allow people to show them through their actions who they are to them, a friend or a foe. One vital piece of information I learned from experience is that no one is currently your enemy that was not always your enemy. You or they may not have instinctively known you were enemies until politics, cultures or other situations arose that exposed your relationship to one another. Don't be mistaken to believe that everyone is holy and on your side, especially when money and resources are on the line. Understand that your contract overseas is not long enough to be in a place long enough to make real changes as a player. By the time a player realizes what is right, the season will be nearing its end and they will be going home. Stay prayed up and keep God first. Know that no weapon formed against you will prosper 'if' your righteousness is of the Lord. God will work it out when you depend on Him. Everything I've experienced racially overseas, although unsettling and traumatic, allowed me to bless others with how to prepare themselves for it and overcome it. Your gifts are not your own, it is for the edification of God's people. Be like Job was.

> *"Though he slay me, yet will I trust in him..."*
> *(Job 13:15 KJV).*

Another point I would like to share with readers is how racism and prejudice are used by the enemy to throw you off your post. The enemy does not care about how you feel about prejudice and racism, the enemy just cares that you're negatively affected by the trauma racism comes with. Racism angers, frustrates, depresses, and brings the morale down of all people affected by it. Experiencing these feelings creates a lot of wounds and unforgiveness in us which is a natural feeling. This also creates a sense of wondering if God is real and why would He let this happen. Harboring negative emotions opens the door for unclean spirits to attach themselves to a person. Prolonged anger, frustration, depression, loneliness, and so on are spirits that the enemy uses to influence a person's free will decisions. If the enemy can get a person to make others their enemy due to changing their beliefs, changing their reactions to others, lowering their standards, lowering their humanity towards others, then that person will start to self-inflict destruction on their own life. The enemy won't have to stop anyone who stops themselves from confronting their trauma. Accept that there is a faction of people that simply don't like you and systems that exist that seek to block people from succeeding, but with the help of God, all things are possible. This is not a feel-good statement, but a reality because if someone can focus and lock in while you're under duress, God will pull them through that situation. For example, I was in Austria having a horrible time, so I let the management know I wanted to leave due to all the traumatic experiences I was having. This resulted in them having a private meeting about me. I knew they were in the gym when my agent told them, and my spirit compelled me to drive up there and go speak to them face to face so they knew I was sincere. I walked into their meeting and sat in the middle of them and explained how they've removed God from my life due to the crazy work schedule along with all of the prejudices I've faced and now they've even benched me when I've been playing well and leading us to victories. I was very honest and once I mentioned God's name in the meeting, the energy in the room changed and they were more accepting of my situation. God moved me from that team with all of my money, my release to play somewhere else, and within two weeks I had a new contract in France and finished the season in my natural position and I finished strong. God will move on your behalf when you're calling His name. Jesus will touch the hearts and minds of anyone you're speaking to no matter what they believe in because Jesus is peace. If there is Jesus in anyone then that person will simmer down, and if the person is not of God they will be thwarted by the mention of Jesus Christ of Nazareth.

It is important to speak the name of Jesus Christ of Nazareth when the Holy Spirit inclines you to because many enemy imposters will try to trick a person into believing they are the true Jesus or others that will make mention of other people with the same name. As a Christian, when we pray or decree in the name of Jesus, we are referring to Jesus Christ of Nazareth and no others. Jesus Christ of Nazareth is the son of God the Father who is in heaven, the 3rd heaven where God resides. And as a baptized man or woman of God, we are filled with the Holy Spirit (Jesus Christ of Nazareth) so we are formidable in times of uncertainty.

> *"Can anything ever separate us from Christ's love? Does it mean he no longer loves us if we have trouble or calamity, or are persecuted, or hungry, or destitute, or in danger, or threatened with death? (As the Scriptures say, 'For your sake we are killed every day; we are being slaughtered like sheep.') No, despite all these things, overwhelming victory is ours through Christ, who loved us" (Romans 8:35-37 NLT).*

Think about all that has been stated throughout this chapter of bad experiences, some places I should've been and others I shouldn't. Many more situations were much worse than these above but as Apostle Paul stated in the Word of God, we cannot be separated from God's love. When someone loves you unconditionally, they will protect you without question. Although I was in a horrible situation, God protected me. You may live in communities with racists who will try to harm you, but you are more than a conqueror and you will come out on top when you work for the Lord with all your heart. There were also times when I was not with the Lord and Jesus still protected me in my confusion and delusion because we cannot be separated from the love of God. You may have similar testimonies as we are children of the Most High God.

Territories of Your Mind/Body/Spirit

As a baptized follower of Jesus Christ of Nazareth, your spirit belongs to God. Your mind and body also belong to God. But due to your free will, mixed with your enemies' tactics, you are still susceptible to unwittingly, knowingly, and/or forcefully having your territory invaded. It is of vital importance to read the Bible daily, renounce your sins daily, and forgive and repent to keep yourself from being infiltrated by the adversary. All of the above are not just actions that God informs us to do, but they're also strategies to stay delivered from whatever may be influencing our decisions.

The mind is not just an organ but is an instrument that can become a battleground for spiritual warfare as the enemy wants to attack our minds. Depending on the opposition's agenda, the attacks can be as low as symbols and subliminal messages in music, television, and other media outlets or more intense such as sleep paralysis, mental health issues, or physical ailments that make no sense for you to have. The heavy levels of spiritual attacks are hearing voices, bipolarism, contractions (not from pregnancy), possession, generational issues, and many more. The latter can require full deliverance depending on whatever the Holy Spirit reveals needs to be done. Many times, just being obedient and stopping to listen to certain music, watch certain programs, or cut ties with bad people will do the job of stopping spiritual attacks. Those actions alone without an influx of the Word of God, praise music, and so on can leave residue from spiritual attacks from the past so it is important to attend church, praise, pray, and worship God to be fully delivered and to stay delivered. Once any spirit is kicked out of a person's territory in the name of Jesus, that spirit may come back with its friends and try to retake residence in your mind or body.

> "When an evil spirit leaves a person, it goes into the desert, seeking rest but finding none. Then it says, 'I will return to the person I came from.' So it returns and finds its former home empty, swept, and in order. Then the spirit finds seven other spirits more evil than itself, and they all enter the person and live there. And so that person is worse off than before. That will be the experience of this evil generation" (Matthew 12: 43-45 NLT).

I know that was a mouthful, but let me simplify this for you. Imagine being bullied and God sends you men and women of God to come and the bully is kicked out of your home. That bully is upset and goes to lick its wounds and tries to find someone's house to bully them but nothing seems to be as good as what it already knows, and it even thinks that your home is its home. When this bully comes back to see you're better without it and all is good for you, but the house is 'empty,' the bully will then call up its folks to forcefully come kick your door down. This is basic spiritual retaliation that we also see in the physical at times. This backlash is one reason a lot of people do not want to confront their sins because the battles and retaliations are intense. It seems easier to keep getting high, keep drinking, keep listening to debaucherous music, keep sinning because it keeps the bully happy, and like Stockholm syndrome, it becomes easier to stay in bondage because the enemy has taken up territory in your mind. The enemy doesn't have to fight you if you're already bound because you work for them when you're indulging in their activities. When battling to keep your mind or to evict bullies from your mind, you must be filled up with the Word of God and the armor of God must be intact (refer to Chapter 2 on spiritual protection). When the devil and/or his minions come back to your territory (your mind/body/spirit) they should be met with prayers, the Word of God, gospel music, and a host of other spiritual weapons that fortify your mind and force the enemy to leave your presence for good. In essence, when the spirit comes back to your house (mind), the spirit won't find it empty because it will be filled with the Holy Spirit. Like someone who seeks your attention, the enemy won't come to you just once, they will press for your attention numerous times directly and indirectly until they realize your armor and community are too strong to be penetrated. The Bible says if you resist the devil he will flee; resisting is not just face-to-face resisting, resisting is a lifestyle. It's much easier to have a bunch of prayer warriors pray a spirit off than to stop listening to music and watching TV shows you've loved for years. It's much easier to have your pastor speak life into you using the Word of God than to cut off a sex friend or to cut off your get-high buddies. It is important to get to the point where the enemy cannot directly attack you, and when the enemy knows it cannot directly attack you, he will try to indirectly get you to sin through your friends, family, colleagues, and so on. Trying to lure you in with unholy conversations or invitations to events that could persuade you into bad behavior are attacks on the mind. Guard your territory with all your might. We will make bad decisions and mistakes now and then, that's life, but do your best to forgive, repent, and as Jesus says, sin no more.

Moving on to the territory of your body, this one is more carnal than the mind. The flesh is a challenge at times. We can fast, we can meditate on the Word, we can read scripture, we can avoid compromising situations, and so on, but the body likes what it likes and is attracted to what it is attracted to. Many people are celibate due to strict boundaries of not being around lustful situations. This is not the real test; the test is to remain celibate when you're dating someone you truly care for and want to be physically satisfied by. It is much easier to avoid someone you're just interested in physically more so than someone who brings more to the table. Many people are clean from drugs and alcohol because of strict boundaries they do not cross, but the real test is when that person finds themselves in an area where the smoke fumes just so happen to be in the air, or they're offered a free drink somewhere. I remember I played in a league that gave the player of the game a bottle of wine. If the person happens to have a habit of drinking alcohol, this can be problematic. Although wine is drunk by many in the Bible, the reality is many alcoholic beverages can have spirits attached to them, hints at the sign on most liquor stores that says 'wine and spirits.' Ingesting spirits into your body through alcohol, drugs, or keeping those spirits firm in your body through gluttony is widely overlooked. Snares and strongholds come from these sorts of entrapments. Unclean spirits also transfer through physical contact, some as light as a handshake or hug, and others as heavy as sexual intercourse. In any case, your body may naturally want many of the above vices. Your body can respond to certain stimuli just as your heart always beats and your lungs always inhale and exhale naturally. Do your best to keep your territory free from unholy visitation. It is of vital importance to pray over food before eating to remove impurities and unholy covenants from it. Each person has several gateways that the enemy tries to infiltrate: the eyes, ears, nose, mouth, genitals, and anus. It is important to protect them through your actions. Anything a person willingly, unwillingly or unwittingly allows enters those gateways, especially if it's consistent. It is like making a spiritual deal that it's okay to let those spirits in. Watching porn, watching violence, listening to filth, watching magicians, listening to ratchet music and people, smelling drug fumes, and a laundry list of sins that enter through your gateways is welcoming spirits into having a party. Remember, when a spirit arrives at a person's territory and it is empty, the spirit will try to enter. This is why renewing your mind is so important because when the Word of God is in a person, your attention will not be brought to sin so easily nor will you feel so comfortable indulging in sin as your spirit will feel more conviction. As I mention throughout this book, this is not to make anyone paranoid or worried, this is simply to inform people so you can prevent unwanted attacks and win battles when they come.

All in all, understand that God gave you a mind, body, and spirit. Your spirit is less corruptible than your mind and body because it knows the truth. The mind is the halfway house to sin or righteousness. The body is the vessel that houses the gifts you've received from God. Guard them with all your might, in the name of Jesus.

A good prayer for athletes to pray before traveling wherever they may play

Father God, I come to you humbly in prayer, knowing with confidence that your Word will be fulfilled. I am traveling to live and play in _____ (state the place) and Father God, in the name of Jesus, cover my soul (mind/ emotions), spirit, and body from all distractions both known and unknown that would hinder my progress this season. I cancel any assignments of enemy plots against me and decree and declare in the name of Jesus that my way be made clear during this entire chapter of my life. Father God, give me the wisdom and abilities necessary to fulfill my assignment and the confidence to assert myself in every situation that is necessary to accomplish my assignment in this season. Grant me favor in my affairs and traveling grace throughout my journey. Bring me back safely to my family as a stronger, wiser man/ woman for my family. To God be the Glory forever and ever, in Jesus' name Amen.

Bonus Territory

The Dream World

One of the primary places the enemy tries to attack all people is when they're asleep. When asleep, we're all in a more vulnerable state as most people are not lucid enough to make conscious decisions in their dreams. In the dark hours of the early morning, the enemy is busy having their prayers answered against the people of God and nonbelievers alike. Many times, when evil spirits want to harm a person, they will come to a person in their sleep causing nightmares, sleep paralysis, and nocturnal emission. The Bible refers to this as night terrors. When moving into a new territory such as a new house, a new city, a new state, or a new country, be advised that there are probably different devils to deal with and many will try to enter your dreams and visions, and even transfer to you from other people through hugs, handshakes, and embrace. This is a reality along with everyday conversations and a person that partakes in that is not of God.

Men and women of God, along with nonbelievers, will face spiritual attacks from time to time whether you realize it, believe it or not. A good way to deal with this is to praise God both through gospel music or just praising and acknowledging God's power in your mind, quoting scriptures from the Bible that deal with God's peace, power, and sovereignty. It is important to say these aloud or in your head with authority, with conviction. Many times, this will force the ungodly spirit to manifest itself as it will become uncomfortable and thwarted because it does not want to deal with the truth of God. You can command it to leave the more you feel the pressure, jolts, snarls, or contractions intensifying. The enemy (evil spirits) makes these actions of pressure, jolts, snarls, channeling, etc. to discourage people under demonic oppression from acknowledging God's power over them in hopes that the oppressed person will lose confidence or not gain confidence in the power of Jesus over it. Depending on the power of the devil being dealt with, the unclean spirit may leave a person instantly, in a few minutes, days, weeks, or in some cases, months. But that spirit will leave when the person believes in God's Word utilizing God's Word and praising Him accurately. When the spirit leaves a person, it can feel like a blanket being removed, a large exhale, violent vomiting or foam coming out of the mouth, eyes watering profusely, snot intensely coming out of the nose, immediately having to use the bathroom, and even pressures coming out of ears amongst others. An ungodly spirit typically will leave the way it entered the person. There is no set way that God will remove issues from a person, but this is common.

When an unclean spirit is removed from a person, the spirit will try to hover around for a time to wait to enter again. If the person is alone and casts a spirit off, the spirit may try to re-enter with more immediacy as there are no other prayer warriors present so the person is more vulnerable. It is like a physical fight. If a person is fighting one-on-one, the enemy being fought is more likely to keep fighting than if a person has friends fighting with them. When alone, and a spirit is removed, it is important to keep praising God for the victory and proclaiming God's power to keep the enemy out of your mind/body. When the ungodly spirit knows a person means business and it cannot re-enter by force, it will try other means such as media shows, music, people a person commits sins with, or any thoughts a person may have of doubt, submission, worry, or fear that would go against the Word of God. The Bible does not encourage believers to worry, doubt, or submit to the devil, so to do so opens the doorway for an ungodly spirit to attach to a person. When an ungodly spirit has been kicked out of someone, and cannot re-enter that person or enter a person nearby, it will go and get its friends (other demons) to try to make another entry spiritually through thoughts, dreams, visions, media, etc. If these means do not work, the enemy will try to influence people physically such as worshippers of ungodly spirits or nonbelievers to attack the person in the physical realm at work, home, and so on. It could be the people at a person's workplace all of a sudden intensifying their negative attention on the person who's been delivered and causing issues on the job. It could be the children in a person's home having more issues at school from challenges that don't make any sense.

> *"When an evil spirit leaves a person, it goes into the desert, seeking rest but finding none. Then it says, 'I will return to the person I came from.' So it returns and finds its former home empty, swept, and in order. Then the spirit finds seven other spirits more evil than itself, and they all enter the person and live there. And so that person is worse off than before. That will be the experience of this evil generation"*
> *(Matthew 12: 43-45 NLT).*

A key to staying delivered is to get stronger in your walk with God. For many it's stopping sin, for some it's an improved praise life, for some it's knowing more of the Word of God, for others it's utilizing their authority more often and effectively, etc. Think about this in physical terms, when a person whoops a bully with something more powerful than the bully, that bully will go get its friends who are bigger and fight better than the bully itself. If the person delivered rests on his laurels and doesn't reinforce himself for retaliation, he will be thwarted by the enemy. We see militaries around the world after winning a battle rebuilding themselves, making adjustments and upgrades where necessary to be prepared for any other attack that may come due to weaknesses that were exposed in battle. So, the next time an enemy approaches the base, the enemy finds the base is much more secure and cannot be penetrated easily if at all. The same must be done for mankind in the spiritual and mental realms.

One area that we all must understand is that smartphones, televisions, radios, and any other sort of technology that is connected to the airways are or can be infiltrated by the devil. This is known in the Bible as the 'prince of the power of the air.' Consider these sorts of technologies as 'mind control machines' especially if you consistently watch and listen to ungodly shows and music. It is by a person's own free will to choose to tune in to certain channels and stations and download various files. People can be socially engineered to do nearly any sin they give their consistent attention to. A person's mind is in some ways a computer; all sorts of software can be uploaded and downloaded; files can be deleted and many bytes of data can lie dormant but still contribute to the computer's capacity limits. Many times, when a computer is running slow, we have to delete files to get it running smoothly again. Consider this as your mind. Now when we hook up the computer to the internet (airways,) our minds are opened up to more uncontrolled spiritual information that can infiltrate it. A lot of pop-ups, junk files, and subliminal images infiltrate computers (minds) through the airways. With no spam blocker (relationship with God), anyone's computer(mind) can easily catch a virus and have to have its entire processor wiped clean before the computer can return to normal functions. It's important to delete junk files (ungodly photos and documents, etc.) and uninstall ungodly programs (porn, sinful music, ungodly contacts, etc.) to prevent viruses from taking over your computer (mind). It's also important to read the instruction manual (Bible) and take part in the advanced courses (Bible study, small groups) offered on social media platforms or group chat (church community) so you can be instructed to not unwittingly click on hazardous emails (demonic information) that could give you a virus (demonic attack).

> "Wherein in time past ye walked according to the course of this world, according to the prince of the power of the air, the spirit that now worketh in the children of disobedience:" (Ephesians 2:2 KJV).

To reflect, there is no cookie-cutter way to explain all situations but with a good church community and informed ministers, solutions to a person's challenges will be found through revelations of the Holy Spirit. When the enemy declares war against someone for whatever reason, it is typically to discourage or stop the person's progress in life due to the anointing they carry for the ministry works God has for them. In any case, no matter the territory we're in, as believers, we are already victorious through Christ and must act accordingly.

If you're having issues with spiritual attacks in your sleep such as those mentioned above, please read the pastor's solutions below.

The Pastors' Take on Sleep Issues

Bishop Lelton Davis
Mesa, Arizona, USA

Question

For those dealing with spiritual attacks while sleeping, how does a person get a good night's sleep?

Bishop Davis' response

I suffered from sleep paralysis for so many years, drinking liquor to try to sleep, and taking energy drinks to stay up. I was messed up. I remember years of struggling with sleep and trying to figure out a good way to fall asleep. I remember one time I was being attacked by a demon. I was upset and bold enough to say, "Show me yourself, I got these hands. I'm LD, I'm from the hood!" And when he (the spirit) showed me himself, that's when I got scared, my heart pumping. I felt at that moment I was getting ready to die. I remember trying to call on God and when He didn't come to my rescue I began to curse God out. I was upset; I started talking crazy to God. That was my reality check because I was raised in church and turned to the streets. That was my reality check, just how far I had gone. I started selling weed, just becoming this very angry, mean person and God asked me a question, "How did they (demons)

164

get there?" That was my reality check, saying, "I don't know how he (the enemy) got here." But God said, "If you were who I called you to be, you would have the authority to get rid of it, you wouldn't have to call me." It was God showing me that my lifestyle invited that thing in. I stopped reading the Word and going to church. I started drinking and partying heavily. I wanted to go to heaven but I didn't want to live godly. We all want to go to heaven and we all want God's protection, but we don't want to be obedient to God's Word that protects us. It's God's will and word that protects us but we're not willing to sacrifice living holy and righteous because we still want to have fun. Because sin always looks good and sin is always fun to do. Most people think, "If I become a Christian, I won't have a good life, it'll be boring." But Jesus said, "I've come that you have life and have lived more abundantly." Your life is going to be better with Christ but many people fear, "I'm going miss something," and in that, they invite demons to their bed which makes it hard to sleep.

A lot of times, people go to sleep without praying. You've (They've) been watching demonic movies and that demon said, "Hey! I'm going to attack that." You've been listening to demonic music and what you entertain during the day will follow you at night. If you don't protect yourself while going to sleep, whatever we battle with in this world will follow you (us) and try to disturb your (our) sleep. Sleep is the cousin of death and while you're trying to sleep, that's the closest you are to both realms. So, you will experience stuff, see stuff, and feel stuff that you would never be able to tell people without sounding crazy. Because you're sleeping, God is speaking to you, the enemy is trying to attack you, all kinds of stuff people deal with.

It wasn't until I gave my life to God that I didn't fear going to sleep. I used to think every day when I went to bed I was going to die. Day and night I could feel the enemy's presence and I would try to wake up before they would jump on me because they would jump on me so much. It wasn't until it was revealed to me that the demons were attacking me because they knew who I was but I didn't know who I was.

I never wanted to preach; I always thought I was just an athlete. I had no plan to be a pastor or a bishop. I wanted to be in the NFL or NBA. I went to school to play sports and that's all I wanted to be, that was my whole satisfaction, everything else I did was just a hobby but my love was always for sports. When I could not sleep, I did not realize it was because I was inviting the demons into the bedside.

Question

As a person is coming back into Christ, he/she may still be being attacked. What are some things they can do immediately to relieve those issues?

Bishop Davis' Response

A lot of it comes through praying, fasting, and learning warfare scriptures. Fighting word with Word, when the enemy comes against you like when Christ used the Word when Satan was trying to tempt Him (Jesus) in the wilderness. To combat word with Word, when the enemy speaks a word, you speak the Word of God.

When the enemy tries to plant doubt or plant seeds, I uproot everything the enemy is trying to plant with the Word of God. So, if I'm (you're) still having trouble but I'm (you're) a believer, the enemy is still trying to attack me (you) because he still considers me (you) a baby. If I'm still immature while I'm a baby in Christ, then the enemy is going to try to harm me (you) because he doesn't think I'm strong enough yet. Everything that you pray has to operate in faith.

When the disciples were struggling to heal the little boy, he kept falling into the water and the fire. He (Jesus) said, "This kind only comes out through prayer and fasting." There are some demons so strong that if they attack you, you can't wait to pray because they are too strong. You have to already be prayed up and fasting to be prepared for when they arrive. If you have a life of praying and fasting, no matter what devil shows up, you'll be ready. That's why Christ always took time to be alone with God, so no matter what demon He encountered on the road, He could cast it out. Always be fasting and praying. That will prepare me (you) that no matter what devil tries to attack me (you), I'll (you'll) be equipped to handle the situation.

Pastor Charles Radford
Clarksville, Tennessee, USA

Question

What are some prayers and practical things a person can do to not be spiritually attacked in their sleep?

Pastor Radford's response

Talk to God before you go to sleep. The enemy will still grab our thoughts and what we've exposed ourselves to during the day. Ask God to create in you a clean heart and a pure right spirit. And anything that I've (you've) taken in through the course of this day Lord, I ask you to remove it, allow me to release it if it's not for my betterment.

> *"Create in me a clean heart, O God. Renew a loyal spirit within me" (Psalm 51:10 NLT).*

Pastor Radford continues

Some of it (evil spirits) you might not even know it grabbed a hold of you, but it's in your subconscious. Some things that somebody may have said or you watched or listened to lie dormant in us and then the enemy, Satan, will hit those things and it gives him an opening to join. Even sometimes in your prayers, if you're not focused on praying to God, he'll try to join you there.

Bishop Calvin Lockett
Clarksville, Tennessee, USA

Question

What are some good ways to protect yourself while you're asleep?

Bishop Lockett's response

The way you protect yourself best while you're asleep is that you have to guard your mind before going to sleep. You have to pray; you have to see if you can shut any doors that may have been left open that day. Be careful about what you're watching while drifting off to sleep. If I go to sleep and I'm watching a ball game and it's on (a popular channel), there are television shows that come on in the middle of the night with witches and warlocks. And secular television now has shows where witches and warlocks are the good witches. If I'm sleeping and I've watched the game, I've drifted off to sleep, and the good witch starts coming on.

The Bible calls the devil the 'prince of the power of the air.' Satan wants to enter our minds and our spirits through the airways. We have to guard our eyes because the eyes are the windows of the heart, that's what scripture says. We (You) have to make sure we're not just watching any and everything, particularly when I'm (you're) in a season where this has happened to me (you) before.

> "You used to live in sin, just like the rest of the world, obeying the devil—the commander of the powers in the unseen world. He is the spirit at work in the hearts of those who refuse to obey God" (Ephesians 2:2 NLT).

> "Wherein in time past ye walked according to the course of this world, according to the prince of the power of the air, the spirit that now worketh in the children of disobedience" (Ephesians 2:2 KJV).

Bishop Lockett continues

When talking about how practical it is to listen to the Bible audio while sleeping, I'm sleeping but my soul is being watered. That's one of the things that you can do to combat that (bad sleep), to make sure that you don't have any doorways open. I don't think we even recognize how we leave the door open for the enemy to come in.

Pastor Paul Scott
Clarksville, Tennessee, USA

Question

What are some of the prayers to prevent sleep problems?

▌ *Pastor Paul's response*

The spiritual warfare is so real. I didn't realize how protected and guarded we are just because of where we live. We live in a country where you see a church here, you can see the next church right down the road. Those prayers are just going out and the gospel has saturated. I didn't realize that until I stepped out of it (America), and I entered into a land and different lands where that did not exist and I was thrown into where Satan reigns.

Spiritual warfare smacked me in the face when I entered the missionary field. The first place that we went, I woke up and it was just like someone was pressing me down. I was sweating head to toe and I just started praying. I said, 'God, you're in this place you reign over all things, God you're Lord over every dominion, you reign.' I wasn't afraid. I wasn't scared, but I could tell, man, Satan was on me. My wife was lying next to me and she woke up and she laid her hand on me and said we need to pray. We just sat and prayed for God's blessing, divine protection, and use us, this is why we're here. As we prayed for God's blessing, and we were praying out loud, and just saying who God is and how great God is, it was like a wind just blew it (the evil spirit) all out.

Satan attacks in dreams just like the Lord still speaks to us in dreams. Satan attacks through dreams and has nightmares and oppression and you wake up and feel like the demonic pressure is on you. He can't touch us but he can make us miserable. I think one of his greatest weapons is discouraging you, scaring you, pushing you away, pushing you down.

I have to speak it (the Word) out loud and remind myself who God is, who I am in Christ, and where my place is as a child of God. When you're out there in the front, you're going to get Satan's attention, you're going to get all of his attention. You don't get any attention from the back row; you get it from the front row and God put you out there (front row) for a reason. Celebrate it. Satan is on me and this means something good is happening.

Pastor Shawn Scott
Clarksville, Tennessee, USA

Question

What are some prayers and ways a person can have a peaceful night's sleep without having spiritual attacks?

Pastor Shawn's response

Lord, clear my mind from anything today that may have been lingering within me. Lord, give me your mind, give me your rest, give me your peace.

One thing that I found out to be the best thing to give peace is a strong, daily devotion to God's Word. What it does is allow me to rest. Sometimes that's me putting my earbud in with the Word of God playing.

Pastor Juma Nashon
Nairobi, Kenya

Question

What are some practical things a person can do to get better sleep?

Pastor Juma's Response

From my experience, getting sleep depends on whatever torments you. If it's spiritual torment, it must be addressed spiritually. You can't handle a spiritual problem with physical exercise. Either way, you have to find the cause of why you don't sleep (well). Is it because at night you are being tormented, you are experiencing nightmares, or is it you are just overwhelmed with one or two things? If it is dealing with some spiritual aspect, it needs some prayer to be met to counter these particular forces of torment at night. If it is the other way around, physically you need to be fit.

Coach Reed informs

When you travel city to city, state to state, country to country, the spirits in those new areas will see your anointing and may attack your mind. It is important to have a prayer to guard your mind before traveling to prevent heavy attacks.

Pastor Christopher Deletsa
Lille, France

Question

How can people experiencing insomnia, sleep paralysis and other spiritual attacks dealing with sleep get a good night's sleep?

Pastor Christopher's Response

The Bible says that, "He gives His beloved sleep."

The Lord gives sleep. Nobody gives themselves sleep; it's God who has given you sleep.

> "It is vain for you to rise up early, to sit up late, to eat the bread of sorrows: for so he giveth his beloved sleep" (Psalm 127:2 KJV).

> "It is useless for you to work so hard from early morning until late at night, anxiously working for food to eat; for God gives rest to his loved ones" (Psalm 127:2 NLT).

Pastor Christopher continues

Sleep is a gift, and the Bible says, "Every good and perfect gift comes from God." So, if God gives sleep, how can the devil now stop that from happening? But the question now is, do you know that God gives you sleep?

> "Whatever is good and perfect is a gift coming down to us from God our Father, who created all the lights in the heavens. He never changes or casts a shifting shadow" (James 1:17 NLT).

Pastor Christopher continues

Anything God does is forever. The devil arrives on the platform of ignorance. The devil is not as powerful as we think he is, but the devil is very powerful when he finds ignorance. I'm awake because the Lord sustains me. You have these three scriptures:

1. God gives sleep. Psalm 127:2

2. Every good and perfect gift is from God. James 1:17

3. I'm awake because the Lord has sustained me. Psalm 3:5

> **"I lie down and sleep; I wake again, because the Lord sustains me" (Psalm 3:5 NIV).**

Pastor Christopher continues

Write them down. Meditate on them (the scriptures), speak it, confess it. Now when you sleep, the devil cannot disturb you. It's simple; it looks simple but it carries power. Write those scriptures and meditate on them, eat (digest/internalize) them, and let them become a part of you. I had an encounter where I worked all night and then after I realized I was tired I had a hand (demon) placed on me. Instantly, I felt sick. I couldn't walk, I couldn't do anything, and I was possessed (spiritually attacked). What happened? I opened a door into my spirit. So, instantly I dealt with that door. Anyone who can speak in tongues, 30 minutes of speaking in tongues pushes back the lingering spirits. Speaking in tongues cleared the atmosphere, and as I went to sleep, I felt instantly the hand (unclean spirit) leaving. I was instantly healed. In that situation, I couldn't call my pastor, I couldn't call my bishop, I couldn't call anybody, I had to do it by understanding. And I have slept like a baby from that day to today. You don't sleep because you think you are tired. Sleep is not a sign of tiredness; sleep is a gift. We give more interpretations to fears than we give to faith because around us it's what we hear. Fear has a way of bringing whatever a person fears to pass. Job said, "Whatever I fear has come upon me." You fear it (the spirit of fear) will come upon you.

> *"What I feared has come upon me; what I dreaded has happened to me" (Job 3:25 NIV).*

Pastor Nathan Freind
Geelong, Australia

Question

How can people get a good night's sleep?

Pastor Nathan's response

It's important to have some sort of idea in mind when you're going to go overseas or going to college or whatever it is. What is your game plan for staying involved in a Christian community? Because when you start getting attacked or when sleep is an issue, your routine is out of whack. You have to start a new routine, a new regimen. If you don't have that wise council around you, loneliness becomes even lonelier because you don't have systems in place to help you.

Pastor Joey Salinas
Phoenix, Arizona, USA

Question

When traveling to various places, how can athletes get good sleep?

Pastor Joey's response

In the scripture it says, "I grant rest to those I love." Even when you feel restless, you allow yourself for God to fulfill that scripture for you. There were sleepless nights where I felt insomnia, I felt overwhelmed, I felt physical things in my body, and spiritual things around me, and just kept praying until I fell asleep. "God, you grant rest to those you love and you love me. God, you grant rest to those you love and you love me. God, you grant rest to those you love and you love me. God, I bring your Word back to you and I say I want that Word to come alive in me right now. You grant rest to those you love and you love me." When I start to read the Word back to God and I start to allow myself to put those promises in the ATM (automated teller machine) of my heart, what happens is that it will pay back dividends soon. I'm not saying that it's not going to work and I'm not saying that it's going to work immediately. But the promise is that His word works and when you bring it (God's Word) back to Him and you say, "This is the promise that You (God) wrote down, and I know You love me, God," I'm taking it (God's Word) to the bank.

> "It is useless for you to work so hard from early morning until late at night, anxiously working for food to eat; for God gives rest to his loved ones" (Psalm 127:2 NLT).

Pastor Franklin Centeno
Maturin, Venezuela

Question

How can a person get a good night's sleep?

Pastor Franklin's response

One of the aspects to consider is whether or not there is any health condition and dedicating our sleep to God before going to bed is a tool to combat these evils. Psalm 4:8 In peace I lie down and sleep, because only you, Lord, make me live confidently.

> *"In peace I will lie down and sleep, for you alone, O Lord, will keep me safe" (Psalm 4:8 NLT).*

Pastors Sean & Erica Moore
Phoenix, Arizona, USA

Question

How can a person get better sleep?

Pastor Erica's response

When I was in college (university), I used to have recurring nightmares. I'd have a nightmare, wake up, and go back to sleep right back into the same nightmare. It was robbing me of my sleep every night, and they were demonic dreams, violent, about people dying. I wasn't watching horror movies because then the question was what am I doing to open the door? Sometimes we do things to open the door and sometimes the devil is just messing with you because he doesn't like you. What I began to do is I began to play the Bible on my CD player and I had it on loop (on repeat). So, if you can, play something in your ears, either the Word or worship. The devil hates worship and the Word. It didn't happen immediately; I still was having my nightmares for probably about two weeks but I was consistent. If you can outlast the devil, he will leave you, but a lot of us give up too soon. Keep doing it (playing worship music or audio Bible) until it does. I kept playing it every night on the loop and I did this for months and I don't have to do it anymore. I had a very restful sleep without having to do that, and the nightmares stopped.

The other thing we want to examine is, "What am I doing before bed?" Am I watching the news and everything is all scary while I'm trying to lie down? Probably not the best thing to do. I (you) might need to pray, I (you) might need to unwind a little bit and decompress before I (you) lay down. If I'm(you're) doing things that are inviting demonic things into my atmosphere, I (you) need to stop it. So, if I'm (you're) listening to music that completely contradicts what I'm (you're) reading in the Bible, maybe I (you) should turn that off. Horror movies are BIG open doors to the enemy. Same thing as any occult or witchcraft behavior, tarot cards, listening to palm readers, psychics, and even yoga. Also, eastern religions, new age things, crystals, sage, etc. These things are designed to rid us of evil spirits but what people don't realize is they're actually like magnets and they draw them to us. Anything that you cannot find a scripture and a verse saying you should do this thing, you shouldn't be doing it. Cut out the things that might be opening the door to messing with your sleep. Our kids went through a phase when they kept having nightmares and we created a little confession for them that they could memorize and it was based on the scriptures. "I will bless the Lord who has given us counsel, my heart will construct me in the night when I lay down, I will not be afraid, I will lay down and my sleep will be sweet." Everything I said came out of scripture. One of the scriptures I love is, "He promises His beloved to sweet sleep." If God promised me sweet sleep and God can't lie, I'm going to lay down and I'm going to trust that I'm going to have sweet sleep.

> *"It is vain that you rise early and go late to rest, eating the bread of anxious toil; for he gives to his beloved sleep"*
> *(Psalm 127:2 ESV).*

Pastor Erica continues

You might need to pray over your sleep. You might need to confess it, or you may need to have your scripture above your bed. Don't settle. Sometimes we put up with things and we just accept that, "You know what, I don't have good sleep." Why? God promised you to have a good sleep. Let's have a good sleep; believe in it.

Pastor Sean's response

In scripture, God told us to meditate on the Word, day and night. So, if getting it (time with God) in the day is not enough, then that means incorporating it into a nightly routine. The first thing you do in the morning when you wake up is spend time with God and the last thing you do before you go to bed is to spend time with God. That will help a person stay in the spirit and often equip them with what to do in those situations. I feel like the enemy (Satan) gets away with murder, that's why one of the titles that describes who he is, is a thief. He takes what does not belong to him until we get to the place where we realize what he has a right to and what he doesn't. And the moment that we realize that he does not have a right to certain things, then we put a stop to it at that moment.

> "Study this Book of Instruction continually. Meditate on it day and night so you will be sure to obey everything written in it. Only then will you prosper and succeed in all you do" (Joshua 1:8 NLT).

Practical Guide for Growth

This workbook offers Christian athletes practical advice and thought-provoking questions to spark meaningful reflection. Addressing diverse challenges within their communities provides biblical wisdom and solutions. Each chapter ends with self-reflection prompts, enabling athletes to apply principles and foster personal growth. These questions encourage reflection, discussion, and application of chapter principles, aiding athletes in deepening their faith and navigating sports culture challenges.

Territories

Question 1

What is the essence of saying "Jesus Christ of Nazareth"?

_____

_____

_____

_____

_____

Question 2

Why is it important to say "Jesus Christ of Nazareth"?

_____

_____

_____

_____

_____

Question 3

Should we proclaim other gods? Why or why not?

_____

_____

_____

_____

_____

Question 4

Do you wear or use crystals, medallions, jujus, or other spiritual devices for protective, healing properties or other benefits? Why is it important to not utilize these instruments?

_____

_____

_____

_____

_____

_____

Question 5

Reflect on the concept of "territories" in your athletic career.

_____

_____

_____

_____

_____

Question 6

Which territories concern you and why?

_____

_____

_____

_____

_____

Question 7

How do you navigate boundaries and respect the territories of others, both on and off the field?

_____

_____

_____

_____

_____

Question 8

Share a strategy or mindset shift you've developed to maintain a healthy balance between your athletic pursuits and other areas of your life.

_____

_____

_____

_____

_____

Question 9

How can understanding territories help you navigate the challenges of sports culture while staying true to your Christian values?

_____

_____

_____

_____

_____

_____

Question 10

How can you stop yourself from making your sport an idol?
(Discussion)

_____

_____

_____

_____

_____

Question 11

Have you been confused or put in a bad situation due to your lack of
understanding of a culture? How did you overcome it?

_____

_____

_____

_____

_____

Question 12

Do you have freedom of speech in your home/current country? How can you speak wisely without getting yourself in trouble and not compromising your integrity with God?

_____

_____

_____

_____

_____

Question 13

What are the three heavens? What is the significance of knowing the three heavens?

_____

_____

_____

_____

_____

Question 14

What are the keys to getting good sleep?

_____

_____

_____

_____

_____

_____

Question 15

Explain your understanding of spiritual territories. (Discussion)

_____

_____

_____

_____

_____

Question 16

What political territory do you live in now? How does it work? Who are the key people? How does their politics affect you? (Discussion)

_____

_____

_____

_____

_____

Question 17

Explain your understanding of political territories. (Discussion)

_____

_____

_____

_____

_____

Question 18

What do you know of your home/current country's history? How does it affect how you live today? (Discussion)

_____

_____

_____

_____

_____

Question 19

Why is seeing God's perspective in all situations important?

_____

_____

_____

_____

_____

_____

Question 20

Explain your understanding of historical territories. (Discussion)

_____

_____

_____

_____

_____

Question 21

What do you know about your home/current country's culture? How is it different in each region? How does it affect your decision-making? (Discussion)

_____

_____

_____

_____

_____

Question 22

Explain your understanding of cultural territories.

_____

_____

_____

_____

Question 23

Have you ever been treated badly due to your race? How so? What did you do to overcome it?

_____

_____

_____

_____

Question 24

How is racism different in the USA as compared to other countries?

_____

_____

_____

_____

_____

_____

Question 25

Explain the difference between prejudice and racism.

_____

_____

_____

_____

Question 26

Please elaborate on your understanding of racial territories.

_____

_____

_____

_____

Question 27

Explain the territories of your spirit/body/soul.

_____

_____

Question 28

What are your spiritual gateways? What can enter them?

Question 29

Which heaven does God reside in?

Question 30

Which heaven is where spiritual warfare takes place?

_____

_____

_____

_____

_____

Question 31

What have you already experienced/encountered in your life that made you question God?

_____

_____

_____

_____

_____

Question 32

What unsettling things might a person see or encounter while out of state or country?

_____

_____

4

Social Media

"

No high school, college, or pro team will accept an athlete's public dysfunctions.

- Drake Reed

"

"Father God, thank you for giving us a great connection with the Holy Spirit in us to know what is acceptable to show the public and what is not, in Jesus' name. Amen."

This chapter is all about social media and how it pertains to athletes. This section also counts for all athletes of all levels, not just professionals. Social media is widely used but widely misused by many. Understand that as a high-level athlete you are held to a different standard. No matter how an athlete may feel about being criticized, watched, or held to seemingly unrealistic standards, many viewers will have very little sympathy for unpopular beliefs, debauchery, and bad decisions. One of the biggest hurdles for young athletes is to separate world views from not only their Christian walk but also their role as a public figure. No matter what a person may believe personally about religion, politics, ethics, and so on, there are certain penalties for letting the world see you in a bad way. Society has changed, but the game hasn't.

Let us start with an athlete's role as a public figure. Think about when an athlete is in elementary school and how a kid looks up to their favorite athletes on television and other media. Most of us wanted to buy their jerseys, place their posters on our walls, mimic their moves, and so on. As a top athlete in high school, college, or pro, there are many people of all ages watching you at all times. As soon as you walk out of your home consider it lights, camera, and action. If you curse someone out, get in an altercation, or so much as thump a booger in public, people will record you and post your actions. It is important to be aware of your surroundings while in public, whether it be at nightclubs, parades, school, or even indoors with friends and family. Always know that pictures and videos of drinking, smoking, holding guns, having sex or paraphernalia symbolizing those things will always be frowned upon by your employer no matter how you feel about it. No high school, college, or pro team will accept an athlete's public dysfunctions. Are there many cases when an athlete makes a bad decision and gets a slap on the wrist? Yes, but that is typically reserved for the best athletes, and the bigger the fault, the better the player must be. The question I ask players is, "What happens when your talent runs out?" What happens when you get to high school, college, or pro and you're not the best player on the team or one of the top players in your league and you knowingly decide to make a costly decision? Will you be talented enough for people to spend time and money doing damage control to keep you on the team in your role? And if you're fortunate enough to be that good, will people deal with you when you cannot play anymore based on the decisions you've made during your playing days? These are questions each player should consider when posting videos and pictures of their daily endeavors. Organizations must know they can trust each athlete, coach, and front office personnel to not embarrass their logo and make them lose money due to their bad behavior. Bad behavior can mean many things depending on the time and expectations of that time. Each era presents different viewpoints in which the older generations and the younger generations clash, but be advised, society has changed, but the game hasn't. Players are still penalized for bad decisions every day that cost them and their families millions of dollars, generational wealth, and a host of opportunities that provide comfort for a multitude of people.

Each contract an athlete signs will spell out what is not tolerated and the athlete must work within these boundaries to keep their job, endorsements, and partnerships. Do not be fooled into believing that because you're a special player, that you cannot lose it all for bad decisions. People can simply choose to not deal with someone who is consistently causing issues or who makes life hard for them. As a Christian, it is already not good to make posts of sinful behavior in any way or others sinning around you. I played sports my whole life. I am not foolish enough to believe that young people won't do sinful things, I was in those streets, too. Being recorded unknowingly and knowingly can be difficult at times because no one can control what others do around them but a person can control what they post about themselves. It is best for athletes to never go live on social media under any circumstance because no one can control what happens live and anyone can display bad behaviors naturally without realizing it and that can harm their reputation.

> "Let no one despise you for your youth, but set the believers an example in speech, conduct, in love, in faith and purity"
> (1 Timothy 4:12 ESV).

The Bible clearly shows that even though you're young, do not conduct yourself in a way to throw off the believers. As a public figure, you're responsible for influencing hundreds to thousands if not millions of people with your behavior on and off the court. Athletes are young and will be given a few opportunities to correct bad behaviors depending on their talent level, but repeated bad behaviors will tend to cause anyone to lose years of their career and lose money. Bad decisions do not only cost the person in question; bad decisions can cost an athlete money which harms their family. Bad decisions can also harm communities by leading people astray. This is no different than church hurt when a well-renowned Christian is seen in infidelity, gossiping, and participating in various unscrupulous activities. This influences people to lose belief in God, leave their places of worship, and/or partake in different ways of life. Although as a Christian athlete, you may think this is too much pressure, the reality is the only way to not be held to a high standard is to quit, but even after quitting, those around you will always know you were once great and still expect more from you for a time. God didn't make His men and women of God to be quitters, quitting is unholy.

> "Blessed is the man that endures temptation;..."
> (James 1: 12 NKJV).

When times get rough, the thought of quitting may come around, but endure the temptation of quitting. Clean up your social media pages, look at it as a business page because your name is a brand in the sports world and your identification as a follower of Christ compels you to be light in dark places. Your page can include family, close friends, and such, but only post them in a positive light. Never divulge personal information about personal relationships or get into arguments with people online. This is easier said than done, but be sure not to post unsavory words that cut people. It is okay to use the Word of God when guided by the Holy Spirit, but do not use God's words to cause unnecessary uproars. Your platform is bigger because God gave you the ability to be a great athlete. It is important as a representative of God to always think of posting from how Jesus would view your post.

Moving on, we will talk about what is okay to post and what is not. Specifically, posting family pictures of adults and teenagers at family events is okay. I say adults and teenagers because depending on how popular you may be, make no mistake some people will try to infiltrate your circle, leech off of you, or just try to cause problems. It is important to not post your loved ones who are not old enough to contact you and explain everything that is happening and where they are currently. Yes, it is nice to know that your new child is here, but a newborn cannot call and tell anyone they're being followed by someone or that someone is trying to take them away. An average three-year-old cannot tell their parents they're seeing witches and warlocks in their dreams or that a spirit is influencing their decisions. There are people out there who may try to spiritually harm little ones and having access to their photos is a means to do it more effectively. Just like in Chapter 2, Spiritual Protection, when mentioning a person's full name to better pray for someone, the enemy can also use a person's full name to concentrate evil prayers on a person. This can be harmful to an adult but can be devastating for a child who cannot communicate as well as an adult. Not everyone is at a high level of understanding of the spiritual realm and many may think this section is far-fetched, but there are many churches filled with people who need to be delivered from demonic attacks that occurred during their childhood. There are many psychology offices filled with patients who are being treated for mental health issues manifested by spiritual attacks from their childhood. In my next book, I will be discussing how parents and grandparents can protect their offspring spiritually.

Keep in mind that 'you are not special.' I say that you are not special not to demean anyone but to open people's eyes to the reality that we are all human and living in the same world with the same enemies. Just because you are an athlete, Christian, or high-profile person, doesn't mean you'll never be sick, tired or attacked. On the contrary, the brighter a person's light shines, the more attacks will be thrust in their direction. For those with more light, they'll need a stronger spiritual covering. Guard your family at all times on all levels mentally, physically, spiritually, financially, and so on. When posting family trips and such, do not reveal too much information. It is okay to post your anniversary or honeymoon, etc., but do not post private bedroom pictures with your spouse that should be reserved for your eyes only. Keep your privacy and respect your privacy. It is okay to post videos and pictures with friends in proper venues. For example, reunions, get-togethers (without drugs/ alcohol present), workouts, awards ceremonies, and so on are okay. Stay away from club photos, pictures with family and friends throwing up gang signs, or with alcohol, drugs, or guns. Your employer and sponsors will not necessarily share your beliefs on laws and ethics if you violate any contractual obligations. Your circle of family and friends should be the ones correcting themselves and you from posting anything that can destroy all that you've worked for. Keep your page free from twerk videos, fights, and other ratchet and debaucherous posts. Anything you post can be utilized by enemies to attack you no matter how long ago it was. This is unfortunate but a reality nonetheless. Always be sure to be dressed well in decent attire, nothing scantily, nothing vulgar because your appearance will make or break endorsement opportunities. Why make $1 million dollars when you can make $20 million just by dressing professionally? Do not let foolish people talk you out of being more successful with their low-level mentality. You are the one blessed to be a high-level athlete. You went to all of the practices, did all of the extra training, and faced all of the scrutiny. There is a small window of opportunity to capitalize on being an athlete, so make wise decisions.

Lastly, do not make decisions that thwart your Christian beliefs. This will be difficult at times because the game is so cold. I once asked an American professional coach, "How do you keep your Christian values when the game puts you in cold situations?" He told me that's a tough question, he thought about it for a while and just said not to do anything to compromise your spiritual consciousness. This pertains to the times and situations. For example, there can be a movement that engulfs the entire country and the majority of people may accept this movement as their own. This movement may be in total opposition to your walk as a Christian, but you're forced to answer questions about it in a press conference as it somehow affects a teammate or your city at large. Do you publicly take the position of the world against God or vice versa? Both actions can have harsh consequences. The game is the game and it's a cold world, even when it's hot outside. When in doubt, contact the Holy Spirit in the name of Jesus. Have no fear that the Lord will protect you and yours at all times. It is a must to practice the laws of protection daily such as prayer and actions to keep yourself and loved ones safe from the enemy and disasters, in the name of Jesus.

Practical Guide for Growth

This workbook offers Christian athletes practical advice and thought-provoking questions to spark meaningful reflection. Addressing diverse challenges within their communities provides biblical wisdom and solutions. Each chapter ends with self-reflection prompts, enabling athletes to apply principles and foster personal growth. These questions encourage reflection, discussion, and application of chapter principles, aiding athletes in deepening their faith and navigating sports culture challenges.

Social Media

Question 1

How do you use social media as a platform to share your faith and values as a Christian athlete?

_____

_____

_____

_____

_____

Question 2

Reflect on the impact of social media on your mental health and self-image as an athlete. How do you maintain a healthy relationship with social media?

_____

_____

_____

_____

_____

Question 3

Discuss a time when you faced criticism or backlash on social media for your Christian beliefs.

_____

_____

_____

_____

_____

Question 4

How did you respond, and what did you learn from the experience?

_____

_____

Question 5

Reflect on your use of social media as a Christian athlete. How do you ensure that your online presence reflects your faith and values?

Question 6

Discuss the impact of social media on your mental health and performance as an athlete. How do you manage social media use effectively?

Question 7

Share a strategy you've implemented to use social media as a platform for positive influence and inspiration as a Christian athlete.

_____

_____

_____

_____

_____

Question 8

Explain your role as a follower/believer of Christ's public figure.

_____

_____

_____

_____

_____

Question 9

What can happen if you make unsavory posts online or dress inappropriately?

_____

_____

_____

_____

_____

_____

Question 10

How can you hurt the youth and your family if you're not being responsible on social media?

_____

_____

_____

_____

_____

5

Signing a Contract

"

*You must be honest and know your value
in the open market.*

– Drake Reed

"

"Holy Spirit, in the name of Jesus, thank
you for showing us (me) what we (I) need
to know about each deal we're proposed,
and the key people involved in each
contract. Amen."

Hiring an Agent

B efore signing a contract, things need to be in order. As a rookie, you will almost certainly need an agent. There may be a few exceptions depending on the greatness of the player and the need of a particular athlete, but in 99% of the cases, you won't be that guy coming out of high school or college. Players who do their own contracts are typically veteran players who have a credible resume and know the business of sports. Representing yourself is very risky. As an athlete, the majority of your attention needs to be on keeping your body and skillset at its maximum level and reviewing contracts, negotiating with teams, and attending agent events is typically not something that players are privy to. The business life of an agent can be shady. If you don't believe me, ask one of them and they will tell you a litany of stories of how people screwed them over. Ask any player and they will tell you a litany of complaints about an agency as well. The only players happy with their agents are the ones who consistently get their market value every year and even that can be challenging because so many people are prone to greed and/or they're unrealistic about their value in the open market. Athletes will also need a legal team that understands foreign and domestic contracts to review their deals to make sure they don't sign anything ridiculous. Be assured from someone who's signed a lot of overseas contracts that some deals have ridiculous obligations in them. A legal team may be a part of the sports agency you're working with. If this is the case, that is a bonus.

Now step 1, hiring an agent. You must be honest and know your value in the open market. It is also important to know your end game and where you want to be when your career is over. An all-conference Division 1 player's market is different from a Division 2 all-American player's market. An athlete's size, stats, and playing style are all factors in their worth on the open market. Be honest about your game. We all think we are better than what we are which is a reason we've become great players, but be objective when looking at your worth on the open market.

An athlete's high school or college position may not be their pro position. Knowing the position you'll be playing and the comparisons to athletes at that position are some things to look at. Which agent represents players with your resume and puts players like you in good markets are the questions you need answers to. If the end game is to play in the highest levels whether it be the NBA, Euroleague, National Football League, National Hockey League, and so on, then your agent needs to be already representing players in those leagues. Even if you need to go international or Gatorade League or Overtime Elite League first, your agent typically needs to have players in these markets and proven to place them in the leagues you're looking to be in. My background is basketball, but other sports will have some similarities. An agent should have a list of players that a prospect can personally contact and ask them questions about an agent's integrity, qualifications, connections, and how that agent helped build their careers. If the agent you're thinking about doesn't have this sort of community, then this may not be a solid agent. There are situations when an agent is new in the game and has a surefire pro that gets them into the game, but these are exceptions. Athletes, keep in mind your level, so if you're a rookie, does this agent thrive in helping rookies and young pros establish a good career? If you're a veteran, does this agent get his/her players the highest contracts per their player's market value? Ask questions, not just to the agent but the players the agent represents. Talk to more than one player in the agency because some players aren't honest and many don't understand the business side of it until later in their careers. Ask veteran players who've played five plus years in the pros. Also pay attention to the markets, not just what people are paying but what positions thrive in a particular country. For example, in my career, stretch 4s who can shoot the 3-point shot thrive in most European countries, and undersized point guards who can shoot and are shifty do very well in most European countries. Role players who fit a role tend to do better in European or South American countries because they're not dependent on scoring at the same level as Asian or Middle Eastern countries. If you're going to play in Asia or the Middle East, nine times out of ten your role will be to score and score big so being a solid role player without being a big scorer doesn't fit so well.

Pay attention to trends. For example, in my first three years as a pro, overseas teams wanted guys who could score, so you could be a guard who couldn't shoot well as long as you could get buckets. When I got to age 25, it was like a light switch went off and if you couldn't shoot the 3, your career was over. Now in today's game, even bigs are expected to hit 3s. In any case, your agent will be the one studying these trends and markets and placing your profile in various places. An agent should have a pipeline of placing players in starter leagues and moving them into bigger leagues if playing internationally is the option. If an athlete is going straight into the top league in their sport, the agent should have a resume of building players' careers from rookie salaries to big-time contracts. When I say a starter league, I'm referring to a 2nd division or average 1st division league in that an athlete can play their way into a bigger league with more money. It is typical for a lot of rookies and young pros to start in a starter league and play their way into top leagues with bigger money. As a young pro, if you're not going straight into the NBA, NFL, NHL, MLB, etc., then you'll probably be signing a starter contract if your talent and agent are good. For an international rookie basketball player with a Division 1 all-conference resume from a good school, a typical starter contract will be roughly $50,000-$100,000 for the season depending on your market value. With one or two good seasons on deals like this in good leagues, a $60,000 deal will multiply into $100,000-$250,000 depending on what happens in the market. The same happens at 250k to 750k and can multiply into millions depending on a player's value in the market. It is key to have an agent that is willing to push for your market value and not bend to the team's wants because the agent wants to keep a good relationship with the team. Although relationships help the agent, it doesn't help the athlete for the agent to settle for less. Many times, if an agent doesn't travel to various countries doing business for clients, then the agent is not big enough and will miss out on a lot of deals because agents travel frequently to various games and events to get deals done. From experience, an agent will be responsible for roughly 50% of how an athlete's career goes. Half is the performance of the athlete and the other half is the agent's performance. It is common to see countless players make much less money than players that are much lesser players who have better agents. Your agent needs to have enough juice (influence) to make a team treat you right. Throughout a season, bad things will happen periodically such as losing a tough game, hitting a slump, or coaching or team decisions that affect the player. In many cases, the agent cannot control what happens but a strong agent will have enough influence to get all of your money, flights, and medical things handled (if you're injured) upon a release or debacle. Know that it's your responsibility to be a good client. Agents fire players, too. No agent wants to waste their time dealing with an athlete's nonsense. If an athlete costs their agent money, they'd better be a high-level player. Players make agents lose money by getting cut for violating team rules, losing endorsements for violating company policies, not signing obvious deals, and just being irresponsible and flagrantly disagreeable.

To make hiring an agent simpler, focus on these keys:

- Qualified (has players in various good leagues with good contracts)

- Integrity (has great character and cares about his/her players)

- Knows the sport/markets (puts players in positions that you have a higher chance of succeeding)

Always ask the Holy Spirit to show you the right agent for you. Make your wants and desires known to the Lord.

Self-Representation

Moving on, let us talk about representing yourself. This is similar whether representing yourself at home or abroad. This can be done well if an athlete knows the business, is elite, and has thick skin. Unfortunately, more times than not this way of doing things has a time limit because the intensity and setbacks can be too much to bear.

The issues of representing yourself are very costly. One is not having intimate relationships with general managers, presidents, and coaches in the vast markets around the world. Another is the time it takes to be a great agent interferes with the time it takes to become or maintain being a great player. An athlete must be around the clock ready to perform, eating right, training right, and so on. An agent needs to be in the cities and venues where events are held where handshake deals are being made such as camps, major tournaments, summer leagues, combines, and so on. As a player, it is difficult to be at all of these events for business as you're in the beginning or middle of your career and preparing for the next season. Also, representing yourself comes with hearing harsh truths about your value and skill level as a player. Many athletes cannot take these sorts of criticisms and focus on the deal until later in their career when there have been enough hardships to not focus on other's opinions. The biggest problem from what I've seen from players who've represented themselves is the lack of protection having an agency's protection when things go wrong during a season. For example, if a team decides to move on from you and you're in another country, the moment can be very emotional, frustrating, and scary depending on the circumstances of your release. Some places are dangerous, some organizations are corrupt, and sometimes bridges will be burned unavoidably. Having a good agent during times of duress in an athlete's career will help them think more clearly, and get out of countries safely, and in many cases, if they're respected enough, the athlete will leave with all of their money. There is a litany of tasks that have to be completed during a roster change that young pros simply won't know anything about until it happens, but an experienced agent will know this and cover them. Know and understand that any mishap during negotiations will cost you money immediately. There are many ungodly people in the sports world, so never think your belief and practice in holy activities will change the reality that you must know the business and have a strong team to not be taken advantage of. There may also be times when if a player proves to be a good self-representative, certain teams may refuse to negotiate with them due to the threat of other agents not offering teams their players because other agents may not like the idea of players representing themselves as it removes their influence. This may all seem a bit unfair, shady, or whatever negative thought comes to mind, but I'll say it once and I'll say it again, "It's a cold game."

Lawyers

One integral part of your team needs to be a team of lawyers. Some lawyers need to reside in your home country and others in the country you're living in. Your lawyers should not have any affiliation with your team so their motives are pure and for you directly. Some sports agencies have lawyers and some agents are lawyers, if this is the case, they're all the better. As a young pro, it is important to have a legal eye to look at your contracts, especially one who understands foreign markets. Lawyers have different specialties so be sure your lawyer deals with pro contracts foreign and domestic. Your lawyer needs to be affordable for you but also have enough power and respect to where people fear the mention of their name. This will be an added layer of protection for you. There will also be player's unions in certain leagues that can be good to join. If the fees are reasonable and the testimonies are real, then pay the fee and be protected. The importance of the domestic lawyer is because there may be times in your career when a team decides not to honor your contract or a team may do some unscrupulous things to force you into some bad decisions and having a local lawyer who understands that culture and his influence can be beneficial in leaving with all of your money. As a public figure, different sorts of financial situations, accusations, mistakes, and/ or bad decisions by themselves or others may put an athlete in a position to need different sorts of lawyers to combat various lawsuits.

Practical Guide for Growth

This workbook offers Christian athletes practical advice and thought-provoking questions to spark meaningful reflection. Addressing diverse challenges within their communities provides biblical wisdom and solutions. Each chapter ends with self-reflection prompts, enabling athletes to apply principles and foster personal growth. These questions encourage reflection, discussion, and application of chapter principles, aiding athletes in deepening their faith and navigating sports culture challenges.

Signing a Contract

Question 1

What principles or values guide your decision-making process when considering contract offers or endorsements as a Christian athlete?

_____

_____

_____

_____

_____

Question 2

Share a personal experience where you had to negotiate the terms of a contract while remaining true to your faith and values.

_____

_____

_____

_____

_____

Question 3

How do you balance financial considerations with your commitment to living out your Christian beliefs in the sports industry?

_____

_____

_____

_____

_____

Question 4

How do you navigate potential conflicts between financial opportunities and your Christian convictions when negotiating contracts?

_____

_____

_____

_____

_____

_____

Question 5

Share a personal experience where you had to make a difficult decision regarding a contract while staying true to your faith.

_____

_____

_____

_____

_____

Question 6

Give some pluses and minuses of having an agent and not having an agent. Which do you prefer? Why?

_____

_____

_____

_____

_____

Question 7

What is your value as a player on the open market?

_____

_____

_____

_____

_____

Question 8

Name the key areas of interest when hiring an agent.

_____

_____

_____

_____

Question 9

How are lawyers'/players' unions useful?

_____

_____

_____

_____

6

Right Now

"

You do not ever want to be in a country when unrest or war breaks out!!!

— Drake Reed

"

"Holy Spirit, in the name of Jesus, thank you for giving us (me) great discernment when people are conversing with us (me), to understand what they're saying to us (me) and what they're not saying to us (me). Amen."

The words, 'right now,' when traveling CANNOT be overlooked under any circumstances. Anytime you're contacting someone overseas and you ask them how the safety is in a particular country and the person responding puts 'right now' on the end of it, it means the country is probably very dangerous and disproportionately too peaceful. I can remember in my career contacting players who've played in certain cities or countries and asking them how the safety is to be sure I'd be okay and sometimes guys would say, "It was cool. Things can get wild, but it's safe 'right now,' so you should be good." Let me tell you from the experience of being in a country with civil unrest, "YOU DO NOT EVER WANT TO BE IN A COUNTRY WHEN UNREST OR WAR BREAKS OUT!!!" Being in a foreign country and having unrest in the city is as real as it gets. Peaceful protests like we have in America are not so peaceful outside of America. Some places can be lawless or have citizens with a vendetta against foreigners. This all depends on what the unrest issues are about and the mentality of the people in the country. I've been in a country where the airport shut down, we needed team escorts to leave the city, and a myriad of traumatic events based on not knowing how serious things can get. Do your best to not put yourself in hostile situations at home or abroad, in the name of Jesus.

Practical Guide for Growth

This workbook offers Christian athletes practical advice and thought-provoking questions to spark meaningful reflection. Addressing diverse challenges within their communities provides biblical wisdom and solutions. Each chapter ends with self-reflection prompts, enabling athletes to apply principles and foster personal growth. These questions encourage reflection, discussion, and application of chapter principles, aiding athletes in deepening their faith and navigating sports culture challenges.

Right Now

Question 1

Reflect on the importance of living in the present moment as an athlete. How do you stay focused and grounded during challenges and distractions?

_____

_____

_____

_____

_____

Question 2

Share a specific practice or mindset technique you use to cultivate mindfulness and presence in your athletic pursuits.

_____

_____

_____

_____

Question 3

How does your faith in Christ influence your perspective on success and failure in sports?

_____

_____

_____

_____

Question 4

What are some indicators of knowing if it is safe to travel to a place?

_____

_____

_____

_____

_____

Question 5

What does RIGHT NOW mean when traveling?

_____

_____

_____

_____

_____

7

Banking

I advise anyone against taking thousands of dollars on a plane internationally.

– Drake Reed

"Father God, thank you for putting us (me) with honest people who always pay and provide what the contract states they will pay and provide us (me) on time. Thank you for giving us (me) safe options to deposit, transfer currency, and send currency

regardless of the country I'm in. Thank you
for placing us (me) with qualified banks
and financial advisors of integrity who
explain every detail to our (my) complete
understanding. In Jesus' name,
we (I) pray. Amen."

There are many ways to be paid abroad. In legitimate situations, a team will take you to set up a local bank account nearby and pay you through direct deposit just like in the States. In some places, the team will pay a portion of your money in cash or all of it in cash. When transferring money to your home country, anything below $10,000 is considered a gift and will not be flagged by money collection agencies. There are also tax breaks in certain countries for sending a certain amount home to your family's bank accounts and it is marked as family relief. This varies from country to country, but it does exist in some places.

If a team happens to pay you in cash only, then this typically means the banks in the country are not reliable so if this is the case there are two options. One is to go to a major city in the country that tourists frequent and open an account there, but only do this if you know people who use those banks and have experience making transactions. Your team owners and sponsors will know about these sorts of banks. Keep in mind some people may not be so honest, so use discernment through the Holy Spirit and prayer to have clearer answers on who to trust. The other option which is less risky is to use an international money transaction service which will take a percentage of your money per transaction. This can be a task at times as well because many of these services also have limits or extra fees. If you're a player who makes more than $10,000 per month, the best thing to do is to wire your money home through banks and be sure your taxes are up to date so you don't face penalties. I advise anyone against taking thousands of dollars on the plane internationally. As long as you're paying your taxes and keeping your documents as proof of payment, then your transactions won't be blocked. Always know and understand that having a lot of cash on you is a risk anywhere in the world so it is best to only keep the cash that you need on you and keep the rest in banks.

Practical Guide for Growth

This workbook offers Christian athletes practical advice and thought-provoking questions to spark meaningful reflection. Addressing diverse challenges within their communities provides biblical wisdom and solutions. Each chapter ends with self-reflection prompts, enabling athletes to apply principles and foster personal growth. These questions encourage reflection, discussion, and application of chapter principles, aiding athletes in deepening their faith and navigating sports culture challenges.

Banking

Question 1

Discuss the role of financial stewardship and generosity in your life as a Christian athlete.

_____

_____

_____

_____

_____

Question 2

Share a personal experience where you had to make a financial decision that aligned with your Christian values.

_____

_____

_____

_____

_____

Question 3

How do you prioritize your financial goals and responsibilities as an athlete, considering both short-term and long-term considerations?

_____

_____

_____

_____

Question 4

What is the most amount of cash a person can take on a plane?

_____

_____

_____

8

Flying

***Keep personal documents and passports
with you at all times.***

– Drake Reed

"Father God, in the name of Jesus, thank
you for giving us (me) traveling grace as we (I)
embark on this journey. I decree and declare
each flight is peaceful, safe, and filled with
good people with good intentions. Amen."

When flying internationally there are many necessities and ethics to consider. You will of course need your passport and license as well as a copy of your birth certificate for when you arrive in a foreign country. The birth certificate may be necessary when getting work visas and bank accounts set up. You will also need a good set of headphones. I remember flying home to the States from Australia during my rookie year. I thought buying expensive headphones was ridiculous at the time and had the regular $10 headphones that everyone used to wear before the noise-canceling headphones were popular. This particular flight had a lot of bad kids running around yelling and screaming and crying all through the flight. Imagine being in the air for 14 hours and hearing the madness all flight, not being able to rest at all. Needless to say, I bought some noise-canceling headphones when I landed.

Always have every form of currency, credit, debit, and cash. You never know what can happen if there is an emergency or change of plans while abroad and the only way to be sure to get where you need to go and have your needs met is to have currency. When in doubt, find the nearest train/plane/bus station and have them take you to an international airport if you need to get home.

Keep personal documents and passports with you at all times. Never under any circumstances allow anyone to leave with your passport, license, or birth certificate. I've had instances where airport personnel and team staff have tried to hold onto my passport and I had to hold my ground to be sure it was returned to me before leaving. Also, never let foreign law enforcement keep your passport or license. It is a good idea to have two licenses just in case someone tries to keep it for a bribe as you are a foreign professional player and some people may try to take advantage of you in this way.

Behave yourself in airports, and don't act a fool with anyone, especially in customs, on the airplane, or in a foreign airport. As you read before about my flight to Finland, there will be some people who may provoke you to act out but know that certain actions will get you placed on a no-fly list or locked up in prison. People are doing all sorts of things traveling that many people are unaware of and the airport security is doing everything they can to prevent any problems from arising, so do not give them a hard time because you cannot separate how things are done in your home country as compared to theirs. For the most part, you will see airport security with machine guns and full armor in most European countries and there will be forms of this on other continents as well. This is simply because different places have different challenges and they respond to whatever the needs of that country are, no differently than your home country. Do not take pictures or try to take pictures with the police or military in airports or when visiting tourist areas as this is not acceptable in most places and they are not puppets for your social media vlogs. Their job is to keep you and the rest of the people safe in the airport. Much of this is common sense but, when traveling, it's possible to see people get in trouble for their bad decisions.

Always have every form of communication available to you such as phone, computer, electronic notebooks, and so on. Use various apps that allow you to freely communicate with your family, friends, and team at all times just in case a problem arises. Ninety percent of the time nothing bad will ever happen, but there may be a time that you'll need assistance. There are a lot of times when team drivers are late so be patient and do not leave the airport with anyone who is not affiliated with your team. Your team should be providing you with the name and picture of the person who is picking you up from the airport.

Wear clean socks! As an athlete, most of the socks we have are worn in sweaty gym shoes and we do not know they stink. I was on a plane ride somewhere out of the country and took my shoes off to relax on the flight. No longer than a few minutes later I smelled feet! I looked all over and then realized it was me. I was confused because I washed all of my clothes before I packed them, but soap and water don't get rid of 100 days of sweaty feet in shoes. Luckily, I had a layover domestically and went and bought some new socks for the flight over the ocean.

Practical Guide for Growth

This workbook offers Christian athletes practical advice and thought-provoking questions to spark meaningful reflection. Addressing diverse challenges within their communities provides biblical wisdom and solutions. Each chapter ends with self-reflection prompts, enabling athletes to apply principles and foster personal growth. These questions encourage reflection, discussion, and application of chapter principles, aiding athletes in deepening their faith and navigating sports culture challenges.

Flying

Question 1

Reflect on the physical and emotional toll of travel on your athletic performance. How do you prioritize self-care and recovery during travel?

_____

_____

_____

_____

_____

Question 2

Share a memorable experience or lesson learned from traveling as a Christian athlete.

_____

_____

_____

_____

_____

Question 3

How do you stay connected to your faith community and spiritual practices while traveling for competitions or events?

_____

_____

_____

_____

Question 4

What are the basic necessities that a person needs when flying?

_____

_____

9

Allergies

"Thank you, Lord, for showing me all I need
to know about our (my) physical bodies'
needs and to place us (me) with great
medical doctors who can assist us (me)
if ever necessary. In the name of Jesus.
Amen."

Before you leave your home country, do yourself a favor and get a skin test for allergies. You may have allergies unknown to you and arrive in a country that has foods, beverages, or elements that are harmful to you. It's not fun being in the emergency room overseas for something very preventable. I remember being in Austria and having to go to the emergency room because I had a food allergy to the milk there. The milk was more potent there than in the USA and something about it made me very sick as compared to the States' milk.

Practical Guide for Growth

This workbook offers Christian athletes practical advice and thought-provoking questions to spark meaningful reflection. Addressing diverse challenges within their communities provides biblical wisdom and solutions. Each chapter ends with self-reflection prompts, enabling athletes to apply principles and foster personal growth. These questions encourage reflection, discussion, and application of chapter principles, aiding athletes in deepening their faith and navigating sports culture challenges.

Allergies

Question 1

Reflect on the concept of "spiritual allergies"—attitudes or behaviors that hinder your spiritual growth and well-being. How do you identify and address these spiritual allergies in your life?

_____

_____

_____

_____

_____

Question 2

Share a personal experience where you had to overcome a spiritual allergy or challenge in your faith journey.

_____

_____

_____

_____

_____

Question 3

How do you cultivate resilience and spiritual strength in the face of adversity and spiritual allergies?

_____

_____

_____

_____

_____

Question 4

Why is it important to take an allergy test before moving to live away from your hometown?

_____

_____

_____

_____

_____

_____

What have you learned?

Write a summary of what you have learned and what tools helped you through the process.

- How can you help others in your type of situation?

- Is there anything you want to add or suggest improving upon?

_____

_____

_____

_____

_____

Through self-reflection, dialogue with others, and reliance on God, may you find inspiration and guidance to navigate the challenges of being a Christian athlete, striving towards success and making a positive impact in the world.

Kindly visit the website to confirm whether your responses are accurate. Click on the answer key available at www.christianathletesworldwidealliance.com.

CONCLUSION

As we draw near the end of our journey together, I am filled with a profound sense of gratitude for the opportunity to walk alongside you, dear reader, and for the countless stories of courage, perseverance, and faith that have illuminated our path.

In *Christian Athletes vs The World*, we have explored the trials and triumphs of athletes who have dared to defy the odds, stand firm in their beliefs, and shine as beacons of hope in a world hungry for heroes. From the thrill of victory to the agony of defeat, from the roar of the crowd to the solitude of the locker room, we have witnessed the transformative power of faith in action.

But our journey does not end here. As we close this chapter and turn our gaze towards the horizon, let us carry with us the lessons we have learned—the importance of perseverance in the face of adversity, the strength that comes from unwavering faith, and the joy that accompanies victory, both on and off the field.

May we continue to walk boldly in the footsteps of those who have gone before us, drawing strength from their stories and inspiration from their example. May we never forget that, as Christian athletes, we are called to a higher standard—not just in our performance in sports, but in the way we live our lives, the way we treat others, and the way we honor God in all that we do.

So, as we bid farewell to these pages, let us do so with heads held high, hearts full of gratitude, and a renewed determination to conquer challenges worldwide—together, as Christian athletes, united in faith and bound by the promise of victory.

Until we meet again on the field of battle, may God bless you and keep you; may He make His face shine upon you; and may He grant you peace, now and always.

All in all, to my brothers and my sisters, the enemy is real and will come against you throughout your journey on and off the court/field. We as the body of Christ, the men and women of God must be prepared for whatever comes our way. I believe I was spiritually guided by the Holy Spirit to provide you with this book and others to come as there is a lot to unpack for the modern-day kingdom of God. I am blessed and honored to be used in this way to help God's people and I pray this book is a blessing for athletes worldwide and parents of athletes worldwide as you embark on your journey forward. Keep working, in the name of Jesus.

Final Prayer

In the name of Jesus, I decree and declare your way to be made perfect in the light of the Lord. May God grant your heart's desires in family, finances, well-being, and all areas necessary in completing your assignment(s) for Jesus. Though our Lord is mighty, He is also compassionate and knows us and our situations. I pray we do not turn a deaf ear towards the voice of the Lord as He provides us with all wisdom, knowledge, and understanding but that we open our hearts and minds to the words of our Lord and Savior Jesus Christ of Nazareth to cover us in places of peace, famine, war, and conflict. Father God, please guard us, fight for us, and defend us against all forms of witchcraft, magic, spiritual wickedness, dark arts, sorcery, and all other forms of darkness. There is much cunning and trickery in the world; so, Father God, please provide us with clarity in times of hardship, ignorance, and naiveté. Please open our eyes when things are not right and keep us surrounded by authentic men and women of God in the physical realm who cover us in prayer.

Let no man or woman of lust lead us away from you Jesus, and let no lust inside of us go unchecked. Father God, thank you for blessing us with the mentality and support system necessary to be victorious in all situations. And thank you, Father God, for blessing every reader of this book with everything you see fit for their assignments in this lifetime, IN THE MIGHTY NAME OF JESUS!!! AMEN!

ABOUT THE AUTHOR

Drake Reed, currently a teacher, basketball coach, and skill developer, holds a bachelor's degree in Mass Communications Broadcast-Media from Austin Peay State University.

A former professional basketball player with an illustrious 11-year career spanning Australia, France, Italy, Austria, Libya, Argentina, and other nations, Reed also proudly represented Mali in Afrobasket. In the NCAA, Reed earned recognition as an Associated Press All-American Honorable Mention, Ohio Valley Conference Player of the Year, and a three-time 1st-team All-OVC player. He contributed to OVC championship victories and holds numerous individual and team records at Austin Peay State University. Reed's legacy is honored in the Austin Peay State University Hall of Fame, and his number is retired at Northeast High School in Clarksville, Tennessee.

Originally from St. Louis, Missouri, Reed completed high school and university in Clarksville. Following his college years, Reed embarked on a professional career abroad, drawing inspiration from his global experiences to pen this book—a guide for Christians navigating the realms of business and life in sports.

Driven by God's calling, Reed's writing journey for this book began when a woman of God conveyed the divine instruction to share this inspired message, aiming to assist people worldwide.

Beyond his literary pursuits, Reed finds joy in cooking, traveling, and helping others. He expresses gratitude for the unwavering support from

God, family, friends, and the body of Christ, which played a pivotal role in inspiring this book.

DrakeReed.com™

ChristianAthletesWorldwide
Alliance.com™

@CAWORLDWIDEALLIANCE

@COACHREEDTODAY

IG QR Codes

FB QR Code   LinkedIn QR Code

To contact or book the author, email info@drakereed.com.

For questions and guidance, go to christianathletesworldwidealliance.com

NOTES

Made in the USA
Coppell, TX
05 July 2024

34300959R00148